Multipurpose Terracotta Rings

From the River Vegavathi Excavations at Kanchipuram

Multipurpose Terracotta Rings

From the River Vegavathi Excavations at Kanchipuram

S. RAMA KRISHANA PISIPATY

AGAM KALA PRAKASHAN

DELHI

First Published 2011

ISBN : 978 -81-7320-111-0

Published by:
Dr. Agam Prasad, M.A., Ph.D., Diploma in Museology
For **Agam Kala Prakashan**
34, Central Market, Ashok Vihar
Delhi - 110 052
Tel.: 27212195, 65688806-7
Fax: 91-11-27212195
Email: agambooks@gmail.com, agambook@yahoo.com
www.agamkala.com

Composed by:
Aman Printographics
Delhi - 110 052
Mobile: 9891395309

Printed by:
Chawla Offset
Delhi-110 052

Printed in India

CONTENTS

PREFACE

Kanchipuram is one of the important cities in the southern part of India from the very beginning. The region where it is situated was generally known as Tondainadu or Tondainandulam, at present in Tamil Nadu state, near Chennai. The temple city has many other names. Some of them are – Pralaya Sindhu, Brahmapuram, Sivapuram, Vishnupuram, Satyavratakshetra, Muktishetram, Kamakkottam, Adipeetham, and so on. Like all ancient cities, Kanchipuram is also situated on the banks of river, Palar and Vegavati. These are rain fed subterranean rivers and now with rare visible flow of water. The present city is situated a little bit away from the existed dried channels, on the northern bank of the river Vegavati.

The history of Kanchipuram can be traced back to several centuries before the present era. The earliest reference to this place is in the *Mahabhasya* of Patanjali [II, 298].

It is the only place that has given quarters to all the religions which took roots in this country. **Jaina, Buddha, Shiva,**

Vishnu and Brahma Kanchis' are collectively known as *Panchakanchi* (five kanchis') or Kanchipuram. Further it is a place of advanced learning centre for all religious sects from the very beginning. There now remains about 126 temples in Kanchipuram and a few more in its outskirts given its illustrious past. All these are steeped in South Indian culture and have won acclaim for their great edifices and magnificent of exquisite architectural beauty. It is always a great seat of learning for various religious persuasions and scholars of different system of philosophies. The city's eminence was further elevated by Adi Sankara Bhagvatapada Acharya, the founder of a line of ascetic thinkers and saints. He established his first *math* here and helped in the reconstruction of all the three main shrines.

This city was ruled by illustrious monarchs from very celebrated South Indian dynasties like Pallavas, Cholas, Rastrakutas, Vijayanagaras, Nayakas, Pandyas, etc. together with Muslims and Britishers.

As a part of academic activities, the Department of Sanskrit and Indian Culture, SCSVMV University, Enathur, Kanchipuram is conducting field exploration and excavation in various parts of peripheral areas, Palar and Vegavati river basins, palaeo-channels of in and surrounding present Kanchipuram town since its incipience in 1999 under the present author's direction. Many new evidences are unearthed from the excavations right from the Early Stone Age. During 2006 and 2008 field seasons archaeological excavations have been conducted in dried channel of the river Vegavati and traced many new evidences related to socio-cultural trends in the region. An innumerable Terracotta ring with in a considerably small area is not only a new finding in the archaeological horizon but also prolific use of backed clay objects. These rings were not utilized for one specific purpose. It may be found that these rings were not only utilized for various domestic needs but also constructed various monuments for after death practices. Terracotta ring structures in funerary architecture is a new topology in burial practice and reported first time in the region or else where. Clay mould backed rings were found in various shapes and sizes from the habitational area in the upper stream of the river Vegavati. While from the down stream, memorials have been constructed in backed rings in similar size and numbers with grave offerings. Occurrence of hundreds of rings in a particular area from archaeological spade is not only a unique feature but also reported first time. Details are discussed as a subject matter of the present volume.

In the preparation of this work, I have been benefitted much by many scholarly works. It would, therefore, be unfair not to record my deep sense of gratitude to the scholars whose work I have thoroughly utilized. I express my deep sense of gratitude to all the great scholars and their scholarly works. My sincere thanks to all my colleagues and family members for their co-operation and valuable suggestions.

I express my deep sense of gratitude to my University administrative authorities right from the Vice-chancellor, Registrar, Finance officer and staff members for their co-operation, encouragement and release the funds in time to conduct excavations.

Grateful acknowledgement is due to the Director, Archaeological Survey of India, Government of India, New Delhi for permitting me to conduct excavations in the region.

The State Archaeology, Government of Tamil Nadu and Archaeological Survey of India, Chennai Circle, Government of India for their co-operation and encouragement.

It is my pleasure to acknowledge Mr. S. Shanmugavel, a UGC senior research fellow, who is working with me for his doctoral degree to his strenuous efforts in the field. Without him it was impossible task to me, especially to maintain the labor in Tamil.

Last but not the least, I apologise to those from whom I have received help or assistance of some kind or the other in connection with this work but have not been able to acknowledge the same individually.

Salutation to the lotus feet of my respected Gurus & Parents.

Dr. S. Rama Krishna Pisipaty

Prof & Geoarchaeologist
SCSVMV University
Enathur, Kanchipuram - 631561.
India.
Email - sramakrishna.pisipaty@gmail.com

LIST OF ILLUSTRATIONS

Maps

Figures

Plates

III. Ram Shaped Sarcophagus

IV. Sarcophagus with capstone & stone circle

V. Urn burials

VI. Single ring with perforation on both sides

VII. Pounding of grains

VIII. Pounding stone with depression

IX. Ring on pounding stone

X. Single huge ring

XI. Rings in two courses

XII. Rings in three courses

XIII. Rings in four courses (granary?)

XIV. Ring Structure with water (Draw well?)

XV. Rings in maximum (14) courses

XVI. Rings in Different alignment

XVII. Group of four structures in semicircular

XVIII. Group of three structures in triangular

XIX. Group of four structures in quadrilateral

XX. Ring structures with outer filling

XXI. Grave goods under different sealing

XXII. Grave goods under capstone

XXII a. capstone & grave goods

XXIII. Grave goods under Terracotta ring pieces

Chapter 1

INTRODUCTION

After evolution of human, he started to utilize the naturally and easily accessible raw materials for his day to day activities. Among all, stone and clay are more common available materials in all geographical zones and climatic conditions which have been utilized by the human from the very beginning for multi purposes. Along with the formation of agrarian societies, utility of raw material was also increased tremendously. Objects in stone, dried or backed clay objects in both wheel turn and hand or mold made, metals - single or along with the combination of two or more different metals, etc., techno-typological advancements and utilizing for different purposes during life time and after death have been increased gradually in the majority of early metal age societies. Among all social activities, disposal of death, construction of grave structures, memorials, etc., after death customs were also increased impressively in most of the societies during the Early Iron Age. Obviously, utility of raw material for disposal of death is varied from the region to region. Grave structures and mode of disposal also varies from clan to clan. Structures in huge poly or mono lithes, dressed or undressed blocks were very common practice in the entire India in general and particularly peninsular region during the Early Iron Age.

Modeling of clay is one of the most common practices in all most all ancient human societies. Free accessibility of the raw material, in desirable quantities, to all the craftsmen throughout the human habitat and the inexpensive nature were such basic qualities which promoted adoption of this medium for a very long time even after advent of metal and other mediums in human society. The plasticity and the softness are other added advantage of this medium. Besides, the only disadvantage of brittleness could easily be overcome by firing the product of clay. After backing the object acquires imperishability or hardness. As a result of all these qualities, clay objects are found in abundance from almost all archaeological sites except Early Stone Age.

The utility of clay objects appears to have increased considerably and produced different objectives for most of the domestic need of agrarian societies. Terracotta art tradition had also started along with potting craft. The early farmers and the pastoral communities had initiated the production of clay figurines probably for ritualistic purposes. Crude and archaic form of animal figurines like bull or ram was the main category in use during the Neolithic times. These forms were hand-modeled and undecorated. The utility of terracotta products appear to have increased tremendously during Early Iron Age for different purposes. The Megalithic builders of Early Iron Age were producing and utilizing clay objects not only their day to life activities but also for after death rituals. For, extensive use of clay molding has appeared for disposal of dead body or mortal practices and in funerary architecture. This category of clay object is a unique example of artistic amplitude of clay craft of early human. These objects are not only in enormous by end of the first millennium BCE but also more artistic and took a very special care in the preparation. It may be true that the terracotta art craft reached the stage of high specialization at the time of the early centuries of the present era.

In clay modeling craft, two traditions are in vogue during the Early Iron Age. One, the making of the pots and pans or the utility items related primarily with food consumption. The second can be seen in the form of modeling of figurative forms which cater to the decorative, amusement and religious needs of man. Gradually clay objects have also been included in the grave monumental activities in the later periods along with or without lithic- protection.

Early Iron Age communities developed a remarkable tradition for disposal of death and construction of funerary monuments. Mortal practices in Indian subcontinent in general and particularly in peninsular India various and sumptuous. Structures in huge blocks, cist chambers with or without covered capstones, rude or partially dressed stones which may be fully or partially over ground or underground, encircled by one or more stone circles and covered with cairn stones, etc., are examples of the Early Iron Age funerary monumental activities in multiple huge (mega) stones. Rock cut single or multiple chambers with capstones and postholes are other typical examples of grave dwellings. Memorial stones – Menhirs and/or hero stones are another sepulchral monuments in huge monolithic. Sometimes they are reported to have been planted over grave goods or set up over or near a burial (Ghosh, A. (ed). 1989). These are arranged either in single or multiple rows.

The utility of artistic terracotta objects appear to have increased considerably during the Early Iron Age among Megalithic communities also. The grave builders of this region under study were produced and utilized terracotta objects in different sizes and artistic forms for either primary or secondary form of disposal of death for both adult and child. Legged sarcophagus made of backed clay in different forms and sizes were in use for disposal of dead body. The sarcophagi varied in length from two to seven feet and two to three rows of legs. Ram shaped, elephant leg and trunk, etc., different forms of sarcophagi are unique examples of artistic amplitude of clay modeling (Gururaja Rao, B.K. 1972) in grave structures. Big pots or urns with or without legs covered with lid have been appeared for child or secondary burials. Pit circles, cairns in multiple huge blocks protection for grave furnishings like urns, sarcophagi, etc., are examples of utility of both lithic and clay materials for grave structures.

Another interesting practice in mortal construction has been unearthed from south India during 2006 and 2008 field season for the first time that is terracotta ring structures. Grave goods covered with flat dressed capstone along with a hood stone with in terracotta rings were an interesting finding in the region. It may be true that utility of terracotta rings for funerary monuments have appeared a unique practice in after death customs of human communities of the region under study. Rings for cenotaph and grave goods with human shaped graffiti and grave goods arranged under capstone along with a hood stone are not only interesting but also a new finding from this region in grave monumental tradition. Moreover, lithic tradition within the terracotta rings have also been appeared a unique feature in the funerary structures. Terracotta rings in the construction of after death structures are reported for the first time in the region or outside and the detail description is incorporated in the following chapters.

An archaeological team of SCSVM University, Enathur, Kanchipuram, under the direction of the present author took field explorations and excavations in various parts of peripheral areas of Kanchipuram, Palar and Vegavathi river basins, etc., areas since its incipience in 1999. During 2006 and 08 field seasons hundreds of terracotta ring structures were traced in the dried channels of the river Vegavathi at Kanchipuram near Pillayarpallem. These rings were not utilized for a single purpose. These were not only reported from the settlement area but also from the graveyard. It may be found that the backed rings were utilized for both domestic as well as after death rituals. Hundreds of terracotta rings from a limited area and in the construction of after death monuments are not only a unique feature but also reported for the first time in the burial architecture of India and elsewhere. Detail description of the mold made backed clay rings unearthed from the archaeological spade during 2006 and 08 field seasons at Kanchipuram are the subject matter for the present volume.

Chapter 2

KANCHIPURAM

Kanchipuram is one of the important cities in the southern part of peninsular India (Map I) from the very beginning. It is located in the south west direction at a distance of 76 km from Chennai in Tamil Nadu. It is situated at 12^0 50' North Latitude and 79^0 – 42' East Longitude. The town has an average elevation of 275' (83-82 m) M.S.L. Like all ancient major cities, Kanchipuram is also situated on the banks of river, Palar and Vegavathi. The main land now lies on the northern bank of the river Vegavathi, a tributary of the river Palar. These are rain fed subterranean rivers and now with rare visible flow of water. The present main city is situated a little bit away from the existed channel of the river Vegavathi.

Palar (*pal* - milk) is one of the important rivers in southern India. It rises in Nandidurg hills in Kolar district of Karnataka state, and flows 93 km in Karnataka, 33 km in Andhra Pradesh and about 295 km in Tamil Nadu before its confluence into the Bay of Bengal at Vayalur about 100 km south of Chennai. The river enters the district about a few kilometers to the west of Kanchipuram. Of all the total of seven tributaries, the chief tributaries are Vegavathi, Ponnai and Cheyyar river. The rivers Cheyyar and Vegavathi join the river Palar at Thirumukkudal about 13 km east of Kanchipuram (Gopalakrishnan, M (ed). 2000).

Kanchipuram is referred to in early literature and inscription as Kacci, Kaccipedu, Kanchi, Kancinagar and so many. The city has many other names also. Some of them are - Pralaya Sindhu, Sivapuram, Vindupuram, Mummurtivasam, Brahmapuram, Kamapitham, Kammakottam, Tapomanyam, Sakalasuddhi, Kannikappu, Alankara Nagaram, Muktishetram, Rakshashetram, etc.

Climatic Conditions

The temperature throughout the year is high, reaching a maximum of 37.50° C average in the month of April to July and recording of minimum average of 20.5° C temperature during the months of December to February. The prevailing wind direction is South West in the morning and south east in the evening. The town gets rains from both South West and North East monsoon. Average annual rainfall of the Local Planning Area is 40 inches or 1125 mm. In general high humidity prevail throughout the year in the region.

Predominant soils found in the area are Black, Redloom, Clay and Sand. Clay, kankary limestone, quartzite silica, sand and minor minerals are recorded from this region. The clay occurrence mostly belongs to the formation called Upper Gondwana (Shales) (report from the Geological Survey of India, Madras. 1991). The town has natural slope from West to East with a fall of 42ft.

Archaeological Excavations

Since 1954, the temple town has been excavated many times by the different organizations and institutions. Among them, both state and central Archaeological Surveys and University of Madras are noteworthy. In 1954 and 1962, the Archaeological Survey of India, Government of India, and in 1975 the Department of Archaeology, Tamil Nadu undertook small-scale excavations at Kanchipuram. The major efforts were undertaken by the Department of Ancient History and Archaeology, University of Madras in between 1970 and 1976 at five different areas of with in the present Kanchipuram town.

As a part of academic activities, the Department of Sanskrit and Indian Culture, SCSVMV University, Enathur, Kanchipuram undertook field explorations and excavations (Map I) in various parts of the peripheral areas of Kanchipuram and Palar and Vegavathi river basins from 1999 onwards and traced many new evidences to reconstruct the glory of Kanchipuram right from the Early Stone Age.

During 2006 and 2008 field seasons excavation work at the rivers Palar and Vegavathi near Kanchipuram by the present author is the subject matter for the present volume.

Panchakanchi

Jaina, Buddha, Shiva, Vishnu and Brahma Kanchis' are collectively known as *Panchakanchi* (five kanchis') or Kanchipuram and it is one of the important centre from the very beginning in southern part of India. This is the only place that has given quarters to all the religions (Jainism, Buddhism, Saivism, Vaishnavism and Saktha or Sakthi) which took roots in this country (Srinivasa Iyengar, P.T. 1982(rp)).

Table I

General Cultural Sequence of Kanchipuram Region

Period	Date brackets	Culture	Important antiquities	Datable material	Reference
I	Upto 30000	Palaeolithic	Hand axes, flake tools, etc.	Tool types	Singadivakam 2009 & 10, SCSVMV University; Sridhar, S. (ed) 205
II	Between 30000-3000	Mesolithic	Microlithic tools	"	"
III	After 3000	Neolithic	Hand made pottery bone tools, shell objects etc.		"
IVA	From 800-100 BCE	Early Iron Age (Megalithic)	B&RW, Metal objects	Characteristic pottery, carbon dating, etc.,	Ghose, A. (ed). 1989; Gururaja Rao, B.K. 1972.

Contd..

IVB	100 BCE – CE 200	Sangam Age	Ru w. RCPW, imitation & imported wares, inscribed pottery	Satavahana Coins, double moulded TC objects, etc	Ghosh, A. (ed). 1989; Raman, K.V. 1982.
VI	200-500 CE	pre - Pallava	Red ware, Imitation wares, religious structures	Literature & inscriptional records	"
VII	500-900 CE	Pllavas	Inscriptions copper plates, coins, structural activities, etc.	Inscriptions, coins	Nilakanda Sastri, K.A. 1976
VIII	900-1300 CE	Cholas	Structural activities, Inscriptions in temples, coins	Literature & inscriptional records	"
IX	1300-1500 CE	Vijayanagara	Pillered mandapas, tanks, etc. structures in temples	Inscriptions	"
	post - Vijayanagara				

It is an abode of many things, some of them are –

- Buddhist educational centre (*theravada* school)
- Jaina learning centre (one of the *Chatur simhasana*)
- Saiva shetra (*prudhvi linga sthana*)
- Vaishnava shetra (Varadarajaperumal)
- Shakthishala (one of the *sakthipeeta*)
- Tirtha (a place of pilgrimage on the bank of sacred streams such as *saptasindhu* - seven rivers, *pancha tataka* - five tanks, *ekdakupa* – eleven holly wells, *ushnasarovaram* – hot water spring)
- Only sacred city (*mokshapuri*) for Hindus in south
- *Sangam* of Philosophers & Philosophical thoughts

  (Vaishnava - Alwars, Saiva - Nayanamars, Adi Sankara Bhagvatapada Acharya & Advita, Ramanuja & Vishistaadvita, etc. along with Jaina & Buddhist).
- Famous advanced educational centre (*Ghatika – Vedic, one* of the *chatur simhasanas* of Jaina, *Vihara & Sangharamas - Buddhist, Vaishnava, Saiva*)
- Kamakoti peetham – Advaita philosophical center
- Evolved South Indian architecture (Dravidian style) eg. Kailashnath, etc.,
- Industrial (silk) centre

The River Vegavathi

The river Vegavathi is mentioned in an ancient *puranic* story. According to believes, in angry mood the Goddess Saraswathy, wife of Lord Brahma (some other version, the *asuras* bade) took the river form (*vega* + *vathi*) to run in full spate and destroy the *yajna* of Brahma. Brahma prayed to Vishnu to save yajna. When Vegavathi disobeyed Vishnu's instructions, Vishnu lay down across the river bed and obstructed the flow of the Vegavathi. The Lord Vishnu who controlled the fury of the Vegavathi river in spate is popularly called as Vegasetu perumal/Yadokthakaari.

Archaeological excavation and exploration conducted in between 2006 and 2008 by the present author revealed many new evidences on the left bank of the present course and in the dried channel of the river Vegavathi. Evidences of the river floods and badly effect on the settlements have been revealed in the area which could be correlates with the mythological sayings on about the river Vegavathi. In the middle of the river channel, evidences of settlement in a considerably large area along with a huge temple ruin complex, fire alters, etc., have been noticed in the upper stream and in down stream burial structures in terracotta rings during 2006 and 2008 field seasons.

Hundreds of terracotta rings were traced, some still intact from both habitational as well as burial areas in the river dried channel. From the left bank of the river Vegavathi excavations, a sudden evacuation of the area, may be due to sudden swell in the river has been noticed.

Historical Background

It may be noted that from the end of last millennium BCE, Kanchipuram was ruled by illustrious monarchs from very celebrated dynasties (Mahalingam, T.V. 1969; Nilakanta Sastri, K.A. 1966; Srinivasan, 1979) and one of the most popular city in Indian subcontinent. Bharavi, a court poet of the Ganga King Durvineedhan, in one of his Sanskrit stanza has said - Kanchi is greatest among the cities (*nagareshukanchi*). According to the available records the region was under Thondaiman Ilanthirayan by the end of the last millennium BCE. A few centuries after the beginning of the Common Era, Pallava dynasty started their exercises and further developed this region. During 985-1016 CE by Rajaraja Chola, around 1522 CE by Krishna Devaraya and since 1865 CE it came under colonial rule.

By the end of the fourth century CE, Tondainadu became the hegemony of the Pallavas, one of the major ruling dynasties of ancient Tamil Nadu and remained as the Pallava country up to ninth century CE. Narasimha Varman I, Rajasimha Varman and Nandi Varma of Pallava's contribution to the city were significant. Narasimhavarman I (630-668 CE) raised the Pallava power to a glory, unprecedented in the annals of the Pallavas. Narasimha Varman II (Rajasimha - 690-729 CE) improved the building activities and built Kailasantha and Iravatheswar temple.

Nandivarman II Pallava (731-795 CE) ruled for 45 years and he built Vaikunta Perumal temple and Mukteswara temple. Kamakshi Amman temple was constructed by Nandivarma Pallavaallava. It is believed that during Pallava period the silk weaving industry might have started with strong footing which is still a major industry in the south India.

During Chola's time (910-1279 CE), the town was widened far and wide towards east, renovating Varadaraja Perumal temple and Yadhothkari Perumal temple and continued construction of the temples left incomplete by the Pallavas.

One of the striking features in the south Indian political scene especially in Tondaimandalam during thirteenth century CE was the rise of many feudatories like the Telugu Cholas, Kadavarays, Yadavarayas and Sambuvarayas. These chieftains virtually shared the Tondaimandalam region and ruled.

During Vijayanagar Kings (1326-1645 CE) their viceroy ruled Kanchipuram is the place of kings. Hundred pillared Mandapam in Varadaraja Perumal temple and the main Gopurams of Ekambaranathar Temple were built by Krishnadevaraya (1522 CE).

Arcot Nawab built (1696-1720 CE) mosques during the Mugulas ruled while built the churches during British regime in Kanchipuram.

Kanchipuram is also known as 'Satyavratashetra', a city of many temples, a great renowned centre of literary pursuits and cultures. It is also a place associated with great saints and scholars. The Sankaracharyas Bhagvadpada swept like a tornado through the length and breadth of Bharat Varsha, propagating the message of *Advaita* and *Manava Dharmas*. Finally he settled down at Kanchipuram, founded the Kamakoti Peetham over which, he himself presided established his intellectual supremacy by being enthroned on the *Sarvagnya Peetham*. According Kamakoti Peetham, he attained *videha mukthi* (liberation from the physical body) at Kanchipuram, in his thirty second year, by merging himself in the presence of Kamakshi. A long and uninterrupted line of ascetic acharyas have presided over the Kanchi Sri Sankaramattam right from Sri Adi Sankaracharya (Kuppusamy, K. 1991).

Chapter 3

TERRACOTTA OBJECTS & DISPOSAL OF DEATH

Clay modeling is one of the most common practices of human in all geographical zones from the early agrarian societies. Free accessibility of the raw material promoted adoption of this medium in making the utility items for a very long time in human history, till today. The plasticity and the softness are other added advantage of this medium. Clay objects are found in abundance from almost all archaeological horizons since from the Neolithic. In vogue, the making of the pots and pans or the utility items related primarily with food consumption and other items can be seen in the form of modeling of figurative which cater to the decorative, amusement and religious needs of man during his life time and after death rituals.

Terracotta craft developed in accordance with the aesthetic value of the society. Introduction of mould was an innovation which could produce large number of artistic compositions in very short duration. In this technique, use of double mould is particularly significant. Domestic utility of the terracottas also increased during the Early Historic period. For example, terracotta ring wells, pipes, tiles, crucibles, dabbers, gamesman, etc., are such multifarious production as to suggest the typo – technological development in this craft. The terracotta rings in different sizes and utilized for multipurpose which unearthed from the excavation at Vegavathi river near Kanchipuram are discussed in the following chapters.

Early Evidences of Terracotta Ring Wells in India

Backed mud rings show a vast area of distribution in India during the Early Historical period. From the early excavated reports, we can say that the maximum occurrences of ring wells till now are in the Ganga-Yamuna *doab*, in the northern part of India. Its utility has restricted in Taxilia and Deccan regions. Their presence in the rest of India, central and coastal regions are sporadic. From Tamil Nadu region though reported from many sites but is only in restricted number. But from the present excavations at Kanchipuram hundreds of terracotta rings were noticed in different sizes and models.

Ring wells, so far not have been reported from any site belonging to the Chalcolithic or Early Iron Age Cultures *i.m.* upto last quarter of the first millennium BCE. The earliest date bracket for the backed products was fifth to fourth century BCE, almost coeval with the emergence of the NBPW and continued in subsequent periods and some places even till today (Pande, B.M. 1966: 207-219). These ring structures appeared either in complete backed rings or with the combination of brick or stone. But in the case of structures traced from the Vegavathi river were constructed only with the backed mud molded rings in different diameters. There was no any single evidence in this area that the structures with combination of rings along with brick, stone or any other different materials.

For the construction of ring well a large pit having much bigger diameter than the ring to be placed was dug and the rings were then piled inside it. It may also be found that the space in between was filled with rubble and compact clay. They took more care in filling upto ground level.

Terracotta rings were reported in different sizes and shapes in all most all Early Historical sites. But till today, the backed mud rings were reported from the habitational areas and domestic utility purposes. The structures, lining with terracotta rings were identified as soak-pits, draw- wells or granaries. However, except granaries all well were below the working level. In the case of rings utilized for grain storage were either below the working level, not very deep or above the ground with or without raised platform.

In the present excavations the rings were utilized for different purposes. The terracotta rings which were unearthed form the river Vegavathi are classified in to two categories based on the utility. First group of rings were utilized for different domestic activities like pounding of grains, granaries or like storage jars, cattle feeding, cloths washing, soak pits, draw-wells, etc. The other group of rings was utilized for the construction of structures in after death practices. The second category rings *i.e.* utilized for ritualistic were uniform in size and courses. But the rings utilized for different domestic activities were in different measurements and single to fourteen courses.

Generally the rings used for domestic purposes have uniform diameter from bottom to top. The diameter is varying form 46 cm to 1. 37 m. From the present excavations at Vegavathi river, rings having the diameter range from 60 cm to 1.20 m.

The backed rings have been appeared from the different reported sites in India which are broadly categorized in four different shapes (Ghosh, A (ed). 1989). They are - rings with wide and flat top and bottom with straight sights; rings with narrow top and broad bottom; rings with mouth splayed in a way as to fit into the lower edge of the top and bottom; rings with wide grooves at both the edges for fixing the upper ring into the lower one. The potters took more some special attention in preparation of these backed rings. The shape of rings prepared such a way and special attention in the molding thus obviated the use of any mortar or binding media in usage.

The first two categories of rings have been appeared in full shape at the Vegavathi river excavations. However a few fragments of rings with grooved edges have been noticed in the upper stream area.

The present excavation reports in India shows ring wells reaching to a depth varying from 30 cm to 7 m and number of rings ranging between single to forty seven. Moreover, not all ring wells are excavated sufficiently deep into the natural soil because of various problems like water level.

But in the case of the Vegavathi excavation, so far we have traced from a single to fourteen rings structures only.

Rings made of three segments at Ropar (Ghosh, A (ed). 1989:305), ornate rings at Vaisali (Deva, K & Misra, V 1961: 11) and large ranging ring height from 22 cm to about 1.04 m at Arikamedu (Casal, J. M. 1949) are unique examples in terracotta craft.

The terracotta rings have so far not been reported from any site belonging to the Chalcolithic culture. Nor is there any evidence about the presence of ring well at the sites of the early Iron Age Culture of the last quarter of the second millennium BCE and early half of the first millennium BCE. Mud molded backed rings have appeared only around middle of the first millennium BEC from the habitational sites (Pande, B.M. 1966: 207-19).

Disposal of Death

Cremation and inhumation are major mode of disposal of death however, considerable variation in practice at different time and regions. Burial is the most familiar and best represented form of ritual practice in Early Iron Age in general, throughout the globe. It may be found that the majority of Early Iron Age communities, the dominant means of disposing of the death were flat inhumation in ground under mounds and structures or with lithic protection and special demarcation. The burial structures vary in size, construction techniques, form and chronological position, and distribution cuts across the globe of various periods. Moreover, the variability of the structures reflects difference in rituals, symbolic behavior and ideological meaning.

Dolmenoid cist, slabed cist, chambered tomb, pit circles, cairns with urns, etc. lithic made mortuary monuments and urn or pot burials, sarcophagus in different shapes etc., backed earthen ware objects were too reported in the burial structures of the present study region. An oval, circular or cylindrical pits containing a large urn or pot, sarcophagus in different shapes and sizes, etc., backed mud ware objects have appeared in the burial structures in later stages. These structures appeared with or without lithic appendage at the top or overlain by heavy rubble packing. It may be bound by a circle of boulders on the surface for demarcation. These are very common burial practice with earthen ware in the region during the early centuries of the present era. The architectural features of the pit burials with backed mud containers are simple but fully protected or well demarcated.

Hood Stone

Single or multiple 'Hood' shaped dressed stone slab structures appeared in the burial practices. Carved stone slab in hood shape is made of granite and not carving of more artistic in different sizes. In the case of multiple hood stones consists of several, five to twelve, dressed lateristic clinostats carvings of rude or rough (plate I). These are arranged in a semicirculer without joining at the top in single or double rows. This arrangement leaves a circular gap in the middle of the structure.

Cists with Capstone

The cists built of dressed slabs are the normal type of cists occurring all over India. In this slab cists structures, the sides are built of orthostatic slabs, one large slab in each side in general or multiple slab sides in some cases, have appeared in many sites in South India. The cists are covered with single or multiple capstones (three). At Nargarjunakonda in Andhra Pradesh, cists with multiple capstone slabs were reported.

Sarcophagi

In India the first sarcophagus in backed clay was reported in 1850-51 from Panduvaram Deval, Arcot district, Tamil Nadu. The number of excavated specimens have known so far not more than fifty. Majority of them are of terracotta, while a few are of stone. The shapes in backed clay include - ovoid without legs or supported (plate II) on a row of legs (upto 18 in 3 rows); cylindrical; ram/ewe shaped (plate III); elephant and bovine. The aberrant types of the backed clay sarcophagi are the zoomorphic. In general a single sarcophagus is found but there are also instances of more than one. Some of them are covered by a capstone and enclosed by a circle of stones (plate IV). It may be noted that majority of them are secondary burials. Some of the important reported sites in Tamil Nadu are - Paiyampalli, Panduvaram Deval, Kollur, Kannattur, Pallavaram, Penumbrae, Chinglepet, Sanur and Sirumgai (Ghosh, A. (ed). 1989: 275; Ramachandran, KS. 1971).

Urn burials

An urn burial, a big pot or urn cover with a domical or rarely an oblong lid and containing funerary goods has been reported from many sites in the region (plate V). It may be found that the pot burial under the cairn circles are a variant form of the sarcophagi burials. Grave goods like pottery, beads, metal objects, bones, ashes, etc., of deceased belongings were placed in the urn. The urn or big pot is in various shapes and sizes. These are - pyriform, wide mouthed with truncated base, with high neck 'mushroom' shaped body, elongated ones with globular body ending in a short stem, etc., (Gururaja Rao, B.K. 1972: 131). These urns are in medium to coarse texture. Majority of them are hand made having rolled rim with or without further ornamentation. Further, they are terminated either in a pointed base to keep them in position by pinning it into the bottom of the pit or with a truncated base with different diameters. It is placed in a cylindrical pit. In some cases, over the urn some serving vessels also appeared with a granite capstone. The entire pit has filled with clay. Majority cases, the area is well demarcated by stone circle in one or two rows.

Important Reported Sites

Many megalithic sites are reported in the region under study by the different organizations. Some of them are Kattamputhur, Palayasivaram, Perumbakkam, perunagar, Perungalathur, Settupatti, Sirukalattur, Vaiyur, Venpakkam - Cists and Crains; Uttiramerur - Dolmens; Ullavur - Urn Burial; the Sarcophagi and Urns under cairn circles are reported in almost every village of South Arcot, Chingleput and North Arcot regions, near Kanchipuram of the Tamil Nadu (Gopalakrishnan, M (ed). 2000 : 167; Gururaja Rao, B.K. 1972).

From the river Vegavathi, the backed rings were traced from both habitational and burial areas. Utility of the terracotta rings in the region appeared in mass, different sizes and shapes and multipurpose. Burial structure with terracotta rings is a unique feature in the grave architecture and reported first time in the region and else where. Grave furnishes with in the terracotta rings are an added typology in the burial architecture. Hundreds of backed mud rings in a specific area indicate the large scale production of rings for multipurpose utility. The details are enumerated in the following chapters.

Technology

Preparation of clay is the first step of any clay made production process. It is executed with a view to have good clay. Because, the strength and durability of the object depend considerably on the quality of the clay. The clay is brought in to the manufacturing spot better to referred as the 'workshop' from the neighboring resource of fine clay deposit. The collection of clay is left at a corner of the workshop for some time. The heap is, thus, battered or weathered by ageing, a process called 'degeneration process' of the clay (Murthy, K.K. 1971: 74; Rouse, V. 1989). The lump of the clay is broken and the impurities are removed. The quality of the fabric of the clay objects depends upon this process. In case of deliberate mixture, tempering materials or degrassents are mixed in the clay before kneading operation. The tempering materials such as ash, sand, cattle dung, husk, etc., are used, as these counteract excessive shrinkage, warping or splitting that may occur in sun-drying and firing. The material and quality of temper depend on the quality of the clay and also the type of ware to be prepared. In the case of rings like huge objects, the tempering materials are essential in moderately large quantity. Before, kneading, the clay in process is moistened with lime water. The prepared clay is divided in manageable lumps, which has the right consistency for modeling on the potter's wheel or moulds. In case of the modeling on fast wheel, the pots have thinner sides. Thicker pots are generally the result of medium motion of the wheel. The large troughs, big storage jars, rings, figurines, etc., are made generally by mould or hand or combination of all.

Surface treatment

The pre-firing treatment and modification of the surface of the clay object is done with slip, wash, polish, painting, incision, etc., in leather hard condition or green hard stage (Jayaswal, V. et al. 1986: 51). The slip or the wash is in fact a paste which is prepared by dissolving ingredients like special clay and ash in sesom oil or water. Needless to mention that the paintings were made over the dried surfaces while for engraving and stamping, leather hard condition of the surface is necessary.

Mud made rings unearthed from the river Vegavathi are well finished, both interior and exterior of the surface and made of perfect mold. The exterior surface has appeared with special treatment in the rings. It is found that the surface rubbed smoothly by a piece of thick cloth with oil, when the ring was in leather hard condition. This process gives not only smoothness to the surface but also brightness after firing.

Firing

The firing or baking process of the modeled clay objects were prevalent in two distant types during the ancient time such as oxidizing and reducing firing. In both of the cases, the nature of the kiln remains the same. In the open nature of the kiln, the gases produced in this case are in constant receipt of the oxygen. As a result of this, the iron particles in the clay turn red after the full firing. In the other method of firing, the kiln is covered by thick coat as to reduce the entrance of oxygen to the minimum. Smoke is produced during the firing process by throwing husk, cattle dung, etc. Further, after some time, the kiln is covered by thick clay paste or wet ash. Due to lack of the oxygen intake, the metal particles in the clay objects are subdue and the objects in the kiln become black. Some cases, combination of both these techniques of firing can be seen in the cases of black and red ware (Singh, H.N. 1982).

Baking of these terracotta rings was made a closed or open kiln at a constant temperature with charcoal and husk for a long time. It may be found that due to constant firing in high temperature the rings giving metallic sound and very strong. Even these rings were in the river water for a long period and effected periodical floods in the river, still in good condition and strong.

Construction of Terracotta Ring structure

The construction of a backed ring structure has appeared in two categories depending of the purpose. One category of structures are on the above surface as in the case of granaries/ storage, cattle feeding, monumental/memorials, etc., purpose. The other structures are below the earth for instant soak pits and draw well. In this category of structures, dug a large pit having a much bigger diameter than the ring to be placed. Then the rings are piled inside the pits and fitted into each other. The most characteristic feature of the ring wells or soak pits are the use of terracotta rings inside a circular shaft to forestall the collapse of the sides. In the case of former type of structures, first working floor preparation has appeared. Some cases working floor may be raised upto some extent and then piled the rings. But in the present excavation, granary has appeared on a prepared floor in the same level. The rings in two or three course may be utilized for keeping grass or straw for cattle, are piled on the same floor at working level without any floor preparation. The ring structures after death rituals also appeared on the same working level in majority of the cases. A few (only three) cases some portion of the structure has been noticed in a pit which is dug below the earth. In these cases, a pit dug for two or three rings below the earth and other rings exposed to the open. Details about the construction of the ring structure at the Vegavathi river has been discussed in the following chapter.

From the river Vegavathi excavations, the structures were composed entirely of terracotta rings from bottom to top. There is no any single evidence of other materials like brick or stone in the ring structures through out the area.

The art of potting craft of the region were apparently well advanced. The mixing of chaff and other combustible materials in clay indicate the potter's technique to prevent bursting or cracking the rings while firing. The rings were molded in perfect shape with well lavigated clay and maintained the uniform size. These were not damaged even after so many years submerged in the river water indicating that the potters backing technology and special care in the preparation. It may be found that the rings were backed uniformly with constant high temperature.

The exterior surface in both types is well finished as compared to the interior and polished for smooth surface. Rings which were used in domestic purposes are only in one body structure and alignment that is in straight sided with flat ends and arranged one on other. Moreover in burial architecture, two different types of shapes have appeared in the rings. All rings (except only one case), used both for domestic and ritualistic purposes were well backed in oxidizing condition. Only one single course ring was appeared with smoky body. However, it appeared that the potter took a special attention in the preparation and backing of the ring. The urn and/or offering vessels made of fine lavigated clay on wheel and bear a degree of fineness. The slip has appeared from rim to body portion and the bottom is devoid of any slip. The fabric is varying from very thick red to orange and details described in the pottery section.

Chapter 4

MULTIPURPOSE TERRACOTTA RINGS FROM THE RIVER VEGAVATHI

The site and its Environ

Pillayarpallem, a suburban hamlet of Kanchipuram, situated on the left bank and along the river Vegavathi and around five kilometers from the famous Kailashnath temple (an early existed temple in the region which was built by the Pallavas). It is a small modern settlement and majority of them are weaver families. On the other bank of river Vegavathi known as Tirupatrikundram or Jainakanchi where a illustrious Jaina temple is located.

The present Vegavathi river has appeared to be almost a dried channel and gradually modern settlements are occupying the entire region. Further the dried river bed has been highly disturbed by the water works, PWD, etc., modern development activities. Sand mining activities in the river are further spoiling the entire area.

Pillayarpalem and Kilkadirpur are small modern villages, under same panchayat are situated on and along with the left bank of Vegavathi, while on the right agricultural activities of the Tirupatrikundram or Jainkanchi villagers have appeared. It may also be found that the width of the river Vegavathi is more in this area. The width may be more than 250 m in this area. Gradually the river stream narrows in the lower and upper levels. Some portion was already occupied by the modern inhabitants and the river stream looks like a small *nala*. Moreover, the entire area is disturbed by the modern human activities and sand quarrying. However, as many as thirty seven localities were traced and exposed the ring structures from both upper and lower stream of the river.

The entire work was done in two different field seasons, 2005-06 and 2007-08. During the first field season twenty four ring structures were exposed and thirteen in the following field season from the both habittional as well as burial areas, proportionately in good condition. Many more broken rings were noticed in the entire river bed. It may be found that rings were destroyed by the local people and sand quarry workers while removing the river soil. Some rings are reused by the local people.

Localities

The excavated area in two different field season has been demarked into two different localities depending upon the utility of the rings. The exposed ring structures (37 in all) were categorized in to two different localities (Map). It may be noted that the Locality I belongs to the habitational area and is in the upper stream. The other rings structures are related to mortuary practices and unearthed from the lower stream, called as Locality II.

Locality I – rings were utilized for various domestic needs. These are named as TCR - 2, 4, 5, 6, 11, 12, 13, 14, 15, 16, 18, 19, 20, 21, 22, 23 during the first field seasons. TCR 08 VII, VIII and IX were exposed in second field season. These nineteen ring structures were utilized for various domestic purposes and are in different courses and sizes.

Locality II structures are related to ritualistic or memorials. The second category of structures is eighteen in total number exposed from the both seasons. These are - TCR - 1, 3, 3a, 7, 8, 9, 10, 17 excavated in the first season where as TCR 08 I, II, III, IV, V, VI, X, XI, XII and XIII during the second season. This category of ring structures which occurred in the downstream, are in only seven courses.

In between these two localities, some portion of the river bed is occupied by the modern settlements and disturbed completely. The entire stretch, the locality I and II, is not more than one and half kilometer.

All thirty seven structures were exposed only from the river bed, hence there was no scope to lay horizontal trenches and layer wise digging. Terracotta ring structures were traced from the entire river bed, right to left bank in this particular area. Concentration is more in the middle of the present dried channel. Rings were recovered after removing the river sand. The excavation was vertical which exposed ring by ring upto the last. Except in the case of two ring structures, all other structures were exposed upto the last. Due to the water level, those two structures were not able to expose till the end.

Hundreds of terracotta rings in different diameter and course were traced from the region during the two field seasons. Within a stretch of one kilometer, more than fifty ring structures were traced and many more were noticed in destroyed condition. All these were not for one single purpose and similar course. These were utilized not only for different domestic activities but also for ritualistic (symbolic/ secondary burial). Thirty seven localities [Map I] with spacing of a kilometer were selected for digging and traced numerous rings in different diameter of single to fourteen courses. A large number of rings structures were unearthed in moderately good condition and many more were noticed in disturbed condition. Broken ring pieces have been spread in the entire area in the dried channel of the river Vegavathi.

Their presence in the area has appeared in two major clusters with leaving a little space in between with distant characters. Based on the utility and occurrence of the rings, these have been divided into two groups (Map I a & b). One group of rings were utilized for different domestic needs which occurred in the upstream near water pipe lines (Map I a). The other cluster of ring wells were noticed in the down stream near Pillayarpallem (Map I b). Terracotta rings for multipurpose were an important observation from the Vegavathi dried channel and detail description is incorporated in the following.

The rings unearthed from the upstream (Map I- I) are in different courses and dimensions (Pisipaty, S.R.K. 2009). They were probably utilized for various domestic needs like storage, cattle feeding, draw well, soak pit, pounding of grains, etc. These rings were in different courses (single to fourteen) and sizes (60 to 120 cm in diameter) but have a uniform shape i.e. same diameter from bottom to top with wide and flat edge. Majority of them are intact and filled with river soil and brick bats and other flooded materials. Among all, a single huge ring (115 cm in diameter, 55 cm height and 6 cm in thickness) which is in maximum size among all unearthed and a unique specimen.

Other cluster of terracotta rings were utilized for ritualistic or after death practices. These rings are in uniform sizes and courses but different shapes. The rings which were used for after death constructions are mould of two different shapes. It may also be noted that the second group of ring structures occurred in the down stream and little bit away form the residential area. Detail distribution and description of the terracotta ring structures has been described in the following.

It may be noted that the terracotta rings in this area were utilized for two different purposes. Due to the diversity of the utility as well as their occurrence in different localities, both of these categories have been dealt separately under the headings - Rings for Domestic needs and Ring Structures for after death Ritual.

Rings for Domestic Needs

The backed clay rings molded for domestic purposes are in different courses and sizes. According to the need of the consumer, different shapes and sizes were molded by the potter of this region. Some rings were made for only some specific purposes. However the potter took more attention and special care in the preparation of the raw material, molding and firing. These utilitarian categories of backed mud molded rings are in a uniform shape but different sizes. Raw material and surface treatment are almost same in all cases. Firing technology has too been similar in all cases except only one single ring. Structure wise details are described in the below.

TCR 06 – Single ring

A single ring with perforation on both sides was traced from the residential area in the upstream of the river Vegavathi during 2006 excavation. It is in well backed and with perforations on both sides (plate VI) and an interesting object from the habitaitonal area. The parallel perforation on both sides, may be for easy lifting from one place to other with the help of a long stick or rod. It is in 50 cm height and 40 cm in diameter in upper portion. Lower portion diameter is little bit more *i.e.* 43 cm and 8 cm thick flat bottom. The top portion incurved and sharpened collared rim in 5-2 cm thickness. It is made of coarse lavigated clay with mixing of combustible materials with smooth surface on both sides. It is a well backed ring in reduction condition. In compared to other rings, it is in less weight and very strong. It may be due to the ring backed at high constant temperature for a long time. Moreover, it has not been evenly burnt, so that patches of dark grey and pale red are seen on outer surfaced.

Similar type of rings made of different materials like stone, soft wood or pulp or cane, metal, etc. are very common objects which are used even now in rice or grain hand pounding. These rings are placed on a stone or hard earth to protect the spell of grains in beating with wooden post or solid stick (plate VII a).

A huge granite stone carved in a square (75 cm) with a depression in the center (35 cm in diameter and 5cm depth) was also noticed in the area (plate VIII). It has broken vertically into two pieces. The diameter of the above mentioned ring and the granite stone area are almost similar and fit for arranging the ring on the stone (IX c). These types of stone blocks are still using in hand pounding and grinding.

From Pallavamedu in the Kachipuram, similar type of terracotta ring was unearthed from the excavations which was carried out by the Department of Archaeology, Government of Tamil Nadu in the year 1970-71. It is also a single ring with perforation. But the excavator reported it as a storage jar and probably used for washing cloths (Sridhar, T.S. (ed). 2004:58).

TCR 15 – Huge Single Ring

Among unearthed rings from the river Vegavathi, it is a very huge in size and shape. It is in 110 cm in diameter, 60 cm height and 6 cm in thickness and a unique specimen (plate X). The ring is having uniform diameter from bottom to top. It is made of well lavigated clay and finished with smooth surface, on both inner and outer surfaces. The specimen is well backed uniformly in oxidation condition. It is very strong body with metallic sound and lustrous surface. The ring has wide and flat top and bottom with little incurved top. It is not only enormous in size but also very strong and heavy. Even after so many years under water, floods and other disturbances in the river, the ring is still intact without any minor cracks. It indicates the perfection in firing technology of the potter. The potter took more special attention in the molding and firing of the ring. The function of the ring is not known, but its unique feature, special attention in preparation and in single occurrence, indicating that the ring could be mould for a specific special purpose.

The height of the terracotta rings reported in India is generally in between 10 and 22 cm. However, at Arikamedu rings are reported exceptionally in large range from about 22 cm to 1.04 m (Casal, J. M. 1949). But from the present excavations, the rings are not more than 60 cm in height.

TCR 2 – Twin rings

Two rings in 60 cm diameter were unearthed in good condition from the residential area (plate XI). These are smallest rings in diameter among all. It is in 20 cm height and 5 cm thick. It is made of well lavigated clay with smooth finishing surface. These rings are having uniform diameter from bottom to top with wide and flat finishing at both ends. Uniformly fired in oxidation condition in a constant temperature, hence it appeared with uniform red surface on both sides. Rings are arranged one on other without any binding material and filled with river soil.. The shape and flat wide edges of the rings thus obviated the use of any mortar. These were used may be for cattle feeding.

Another two twin rings (TCR – 21 & 22) structure with similar measurements (60 × 20 × 5 cm) were unearthed from little bit away for the above structure in the same locality.

TCR 16 – Rings in three courses

A group of three backed mud rings were arranged one on other and unearthed from the same locality in good condition (plate XII). It has filled with river soil and brick bats. It has unearthed a one and half feet below in the present river bed. These rings are – 75 cm diameter, 24 cm height and 5 cm thickness in measurements. Rings were arranged one on other without any binding material. These are made of a perfect mould with flat edges and uniformly backed. The functional use of the rings may be for cattle feeding or storing.

TCR -12 Rings in Four courses (Granary?)

A group of another four rings (plate XIII) arranged on one another has traced after removing a two feet river soil in the habitational area. Rings are with 100 cm in diameter, 30 cm height and 6 cm thick. The first two rings appeared with multiple cracks but intact till excavation. This cluster of rings were arranged perfectly one on the other without any binding media. These backed rings were placed on the hard prepared floor. The floor was made of compact clay with *moram* and brick bats but not raised. Entire structure was filled with sand and other flood materials. There is no evidence of chard grains or any other organic material. It may be because of the entire structure was under the river water for so many years. The rings are in damaged condition. It may be presumed that the structure was used for storing grains or other raw material.

TCR 08 VIII – Draw-well

From a ring structure, after seven rings water was noticed (plate XIV). Presumably, it may be a draw well (?). Total number of rings is not known, but exposed upto nine rings. Because of water it was not possible to excavate upto the last ring. Rings were arranged on one another. Both ends of each ring are wide and flat and arranged one on the other without any binding material. There is no evidence to analyse the purpose of the structure.

TCR 18 Rings in Fourteen courses

A fourteen rings structure (draw well or soak pit ?) has been traced in the upstream of the river Vegavathi (plate XV). It is in maximum courses of rings among all unearthed structures in this area. Exposed upto the last ring *i.e.* fourteen rings. First four rings were in damaged condition but other ten rings are in good condition. All rings are made of well lavigated clay with same measurements and shapes. These are in 100 cm diameter with 25 cm height and 5 cm uniform thickness throughout. Well backed ring under oxidizing condition, but were not uniformly fired, hence we can see the black patches here and there on the outer surface. Both edges are flat and wide and arranged one on other. Some rings were adjusted with brick bats. Entire well filled with sand and brick bats without any organic materials. In all possibilities, it may appear as a draw well rather than soak pit.

Wells with or without lining of bricks, stone or terracotta rings have been found in excavations at many Early Historical sites in India. It shows further that the characteristic features of the early habitants from the very beginning. But from the present study area at Kanchipuram has appeared a unique feature and rare practice. The entire ring structures built in the area were noticed without any other materials like stone or brick. It may also be found that the rings were molded in different sizes for different specific needs of the society in large scale. Further, a large number of ring structures in a considerably small area indicating that the utility of backed mud rings for different domestic needs of a particular community.

Ring Measurements

All rings which were used for different domestic purposes, were made of perfect mould and well backed in oxidizing condition (except above mentioned only one single course ring) in similar alignment pattern. All these rings are similar in shape but different measurements. The rings are generally in straight side with wide and flat top and bottom edges.

The existed evidences shows from the archaeological sites of the rest of India that the ring wells have a uniform diameter from bottom to top varying between 46 cm to 1.35 m. These are classified into two diameter groups - one with diameter ranging between 46 to 76 and other above 76 cm (Ghose, A. (ed). 1989: 305).

From the river Vegavathi, the rings occurred with the diameter range in between 60 cm to 1.20 m and height ranges from 15 to 55 cm with thickness 5 to 8 cm. The diameter ranges in between 90 cm to 1.10 m are more common size rings which were used for different domestic purposes. In this category of utility, the mud mould backed rings with less than 90 cm are very few. Only three localities, less than 90 cm diameter category of rings were reported in different heights and courses. All three ring structures were reported in different places in the same upstream area of the river Vegavathi with 60 cm in diameter but in different courses. Among three, only one was in 50 cm height in single course with perforation on both sides which presumed to be utilized in pounding of grains (plate X). Other two are in 20 cm height and unearthed from different areas in two courses. The diameter range in between 90 and 100 cm are more common in domestic utilitarian category. It seems that the rings with diameter 90 cm and 100 cm are more common utilitarian type throughout settlement. Some specific purpose potters were molded huge rings with 1.10 - 1.20 m diameter. A huge ring with 115 × 55 × 6 cm measurements with heavy weight is a unique specimen from the entire excavation. In general, the diameter ranging from 100 to 110 cm are in many courses (11, 14, etc., courses). These were may be used for draw well or soak pit. Only one case, the rings were reported with 1.20 m diameter with 25 cm height in five courses. These are maximum diameter range rings reported from the river Vegavathi.

The shape of the rings molded such a way thus obviated the use of any mortar or binding medium. But in a few cases rings are arranged with some brick bats support to adjust the height of the rings. All rings are in perfect round shape and well backed in oxidizing conditions. The metallic sound of the ring is indicating that these were backed in a constant fire with high temperature for a long time. The survival of these rings under river bed for a long time in different water forces, further indicating that the adopted of advanced technologies in the preparation of raw material and firing techniques of the potters in this region. Uniform shapes and sizes are also indicating the molded technology and large scale production to cater the needs of a specific use of a particular community or a society.

Filling Materials

From the most of the ring structures under this category, were filled with the river soil and brick bats, pot sherds, stone pieces, etc., flood materials. It may be noted that there is no any specific filling pattern or material. Further, there is no any evidence of organic or any other materials from the exposed rings. The river sand filling was noticed in all the cases. It may be presumed form the evidences that the region was suddenly evacuated by the inhabitants due to heavy floods in the river Vegavathi. Because, the major filling soil has not appeared much more difference and with very less flood materials. The rings, even in multi-courses, are still intact. It further indicates that the major portion of the rings were filled and covered with river soil in one time not in different seasons. If the filling could be in different seasons, it is not possible to survive without damage or intact in their position of the structure, especially in the case of rings were used on the above working level in multiple courses.

The maximum occurrence of rings in a particular area, either in good condition or damaged, indicates the concentration of the habitation of a particular community of a period. Sporadic presence of the rings in and surrounding areas of Tiruparthrikundram on right bank of the river Vegavathi indicate their use in subsequent periods for only a specific purpose.

According to the local people, hundreds of ring structures were destroyed and some rings were re-used by the modern inhabitants of the surrounding areas for plant growing, cattle feeding, ring pieces in raising floor level, in the wall foundations, etc.

Ring Structures for After Death Rituals

In this category of ring structures unearthed from the river Vegavathi were utilized to protect the offering deposits to deceased or ancestors by the descendants. After funerary rituals celebrated by the survivors, the backed mud mold rings were utilized to construct the grave structure as a memorials with special offerings. It may be true that the graves represent only a final stage in the funereal ritual in memory of the deceased with offerings along with or without relics and/or ashes. Further, burial is the most familiar and best representative form of ritual practice from the Early Iron Age across the globe. It may also be very common appearance that the arrangement of grave and nature of above ground structure vary from clan to clan and region to region. From the present region, the grave structures were constructed with the terracotta rings which is not only a unique but also reported for the first time in the burial architecture and details.

Under this category of rings are uniform in number throughout the exposed structures in this area. All backed mud ring structures of this category are in seven courses of rings only. Variation in arrangement pattern has been appeared in the backed ring monuments. Different types of alignment has also adopted in the rings structure which were used for a specific purpose. Two categories of backed mud ring were molded for the burial architecture. These are - one category of structures made of backed rings was common shape which also utilized for different domestic need. That means rings molded with wide and flat top and bottoms were utilized for both domestic and ritualistic. The other new adopted shape for only after death structures was rings with a narrow top and broad bottom in a way as to fit into the upper edge of the corresponding lower ring (plate XVI a). These types of rings were not appeared in domestic utilitarian category. However they were maintained a uniform size and total number of rings throughout the structures. It may appear that the potter took special attention in the preparation of different shapes of backed rings for this category of structures. Well backed mud rings with smooth surface on both sides were arranged carefully with out any binding media. Considerably a good number of structures with terracotta rings of this category are intact. Of course many more have appeared in the destroyed condition. In all eighteen structures were exposed and recorded extensively.

In general, the present evidences till today within India or elsewhere, shows ring made of mud used for different domestic activities during the life time of a man. Their utility in grave structures are not only an evidence of a new tradition but also reported for the first time. Detail description of the each structure, alignment pattern of the rings and grave furnishes within the terracotta rings are discussed in the following.

Different Ring Moldings

The alignment pattern of the rings has also appeared in two distinct ways in burial architecture. They are arranged on one another pattern and inserted into other (plate XVI). So the potter put a special effort to prepare two different types of rings in the region. In the first case, the rings having uniform diameter with wide and flat top and bottom (plate XVI b). This shape of rings was very common in the habitational areas in different measurements. Majority of the ring structures were found with this category of rings even in the burial structures.

Other type of ring was prepared with slight tapering at top and broad and flat bottom, thus it can, not only insert into other ring but also obviated the use of any motor or binding media (plate XVI a). Structures with this type of ring shapes however, are in very limited number. Ring structures number – TCR 3, 3a, 10 and TCR 08 II have appeared with the second category of rings. Both types of clay ring models were noticed only in the after death architecture.

Ring Measurements

Molded backed mud rings, which were utilized for the construction of funerary monuments, have the same measurements. The number of rings is also same in all unearthed structures of this category. These are built of seven rings structures (plate XXVII). In this context, it is worthwhile to mention about the importance of the number seven. Seven is more sacred and favorite number and used often in Vedic systems. Some of them are – seven *rishis*, streams, rivers, oceans; cities, division of upward & downward words; planets, days in a week, ranges of mountains, *dvipa*, horses of Sun, etc. [*RV* I - 62,4; 63,7; 72,6].

Almost all rings in this category are in 75 cm diameter and 15 cm height with 5 cm in thickness (15:3:1). Even though the shape is not same in all structures, but the uniform ring size and number of rings were maintained by the builders of the ring monuments.

Ring Structures in Different Ground Plan

These structures have appeared in two different ground plans. One has appeared in single or individual structure and other in cluster or group. The second category of structures were constructed in different alignments. These were laid in semi circular, triangular, quadrilateral, etc., in construction plan. It has been noticed that a group of ring structures, three or four, arranged in different geometrical forms leaving with a two meters space in between each other. All these group structures were noticed only in a particular area. In the case of single or individual ring monuments are appeared sporadically in the entire area. However, in all cases the size and number of rings are common with similar grave goods furnishing patters.

The cluster of rings monuments have been noticed in three different areas during 2008 excavations. Ring structure - TCR 08 I, II, III and IV were arranged in semi-circularly with a two meters distance in between each structure (plate XVII). Another group of three monuments - TCR 08 V, VI and VII were arranged in triangle shape (plate XVIII) near to the former. Other cluster of monuments - TCR 08 VIII, IX, X and XI has been noticed a little bit away from the above, in quadrilateral alignment (plate XIX). All are arranged uniformly with almost equal distance from one another on the same working floor with similar type of grave goods and filling pattern. Structure wise details are described in the following.

Semicircular alignment (plate XVII)

A group of four ring structures (TCR 08 III to VI) were constructed in semicircular in ground plan. The space in between each structure is 2 m. Similar shape of rings was used in all four structures. All rings are made of perfect mould and straight side with well finished body on both sides. These rings are having wide and flat top and bottom and arranged one above the other without any binding material. Among four, one was completely damaged (TCR 08 III) but broken rings and structure alignment was still intact. TCR 08 IV & VI ring structures were exposed in good condition and partially damaged in the third case (TCR 08 V). Similar typology has appeared in grave goods in all four cases.

Triangular arrangement (plate XVIII)

A few meters away from the above mentioned group structures, another three clay ring monuments (TCR 7, 8 & 9) were traced in triangular ground plan. Rings used in all these three cases were similar to the above mentioned structure. In between these three memorials, the distance was also maintained the same (2 m). Among three, one (TCR 8) was partially damaged and other two were moderately in good condition. Similar typology in grave goods and filling pattern has noticed in all three structures.

Quadrilateral arrangement (plate XVIII)

Another cluster of backed ring structures were noticed near to the above structures. It was in a group of four (TCR 08 X to XIII). These four backed clay ring monuments were arranged in quadrilateral or opposite to each other with 2 m distance from each other. Among four, only one (TCR 08 X) was in good condition. Other three structures were damaged upto first four rings. Brocken grave goods, however, were noticed from all the three ring wells. It may also appear that all four structures were furnished with the similar pot types and arranged in similar pattern.

In the case of the individual memorial structures are appeared in haphazardly in the entire area. In these cases, there is no any particular pattern in the construction of the ring structures. However, a considerable distance was maintained from one structure to other. It may also be noted in the case of group structures that shape of the ring is same in all cases. Distance in between one structure to other was also maintained the same. Soil filling pattern and grave goods typology was also appear similarly. Moreover, these clusters were noticed only in a particular area. It may be presumed from the unearthed evidences that the structures in group or cluster constructed may be by the same clan or family in almost similar period. Whereas in the other individual structures in the entire area, even though some common pattern has appeared through out, vary from one to another. Seven rings in each structure are common among all but ring shape variation has been noticed in some cases. Filling soil was same in all cases but filling pattern differ in some cases. Grave goods were protected by various methods. Stone slabs, terracotta ring pieces, backed bricks, broken pot sherds, etc., different materials were used in the protection of grave goods and offerings. In a few cases typological variation in the grave goods have also been noticed in the individual memorials. From existed evidences we can assume that other than structures in cluster, even though they were constructed by the same clan, some variation has appeared. It may be due to the traditional variation from one family to other or one generation to generation.

Construction of Ring Monuments

Majority of the ring structures were constructed on the above ground level. It may also be noted that there was no any special preparation of the ground before arrange the rings. Only two structures (TCR 10 & 17) were noticed below the ground level. First two rings have appeared in a pit which was dug below the working level. The rings were arranged one above the other with out any binding material. Further, the entire rings were not arranged at a time. It is quite possible that the first three or four rings were placed at a time and filled with special soil upto two rings and furnished with the grave offerings. The offering vessels were covered with either pot sherds or another vessel. In a few cases, a special protection has also appeared to cover the grave furnishes. However in over all a special protection of offering vessels has appeared in the ring structures. Remaining other rings were arranged after rituals. The entire structure was tightly packed with the same soil.

Filling pattern of Ring Monuments

Ring structures constructed in memory of the deceased appeared with a special fill pattern. These were filled with an exceptional care and packed tightly with soil, hence the flood material were not entered in the structure. Moreover, in all ring monuments unearthed from the areas were showing extraordinary filling patter with a particular soil. Similar soil which is not a local deposit has also appeared in all most all cases, except in three ring structures. However, all these structures were extensively damaged. It may be possible that the erosion of the original soil in the structures and replaced with river soil due to the floods and stream force. Through out seven courses ring structure were filled uniformly with similar type of soil. Grayish compact clay with fine sand, which is not a local deposit, filled from the bottom to top with domical shape on the surface. It may appear that first two rings from the bottom first filled with soil and grave offerings were placed on the soil in two or three layers. Between third/fourth and sixth course of the rings from the bottom, funerary goods were furnished. In some cases grave goods were covered or sealed with stone slabs, terracotta ring pieces, etc., in fifth ring (discussed in the below). In between third and fifth or sixth rings grave goods with filling soil has been appeared in most of the cases. Sixth and seventh rings were filled again with the same soil. Domical roof finishing has appeared on the top of the seventh ring (plate XX).

Sealing or covering on grave goods

Another interesting observation from ring monuments is sealing the grave goods. Majority of them are appeared without sealing or any special protection to the grave goods. In these cases, similar soil filling pattern has appeared throughout, from bottom to top with grave goods in the middle. After filling soil upto third ring, furnished with grave goods in between third and fourth or fifth rings in two layers. After completion of offerings, they filled with soil upto seventh ring. In most of the structures, there is no demarcation or special protection to offering vessels. However, they took special care to cover the offering vessels. The food offering vessels were placed in a big half broken pot (plate XXXIII). It may also found that vessels (spouted with round base) for liquid offerings were placed on rims of a body portion removed pots as a stand (plate XXXIV). It indicates their special care in keeping the pot in straight position to over comes the spill of liquid. All these vessels with in the rings were coved with either broken pot pieces (plate XXXI) or inverted another broken pot (plate XXVIII) or placed another offering vessel. In one case TCR 3, a flat thin brick has coved a cooking vessel (plate XXXII). It is almost square in shape and thin section (18 × 18 × 4 cm). It may be to avoid tampering other particles into the vessels which contain food offerings while the filling the monument with soil or later. In only one case the cooking vessel was covered with a lid (may be lamp?). It is a well backed red ware lid with heavy weight in 15 cm diameter.

Special protection to grave goods with in the rings

In a few cases, a special care has appeared in protecting the grave goods and food offerings with in the ring monuments. After ritual ceremony, they covered the grave furnishes with some other material before filling with soil. It was also noticed that dressed stone slabs and terracotta ring pieces were rarely used to cover the grave goods. In the third ring from the top, a well dressed flat stone slab and hood shape carved sand stone have recovered from only one monument. In a few cases (three in all) terracotta broken ring pieces were recovered in two layers, just above on the grave goods.

It may be found that they adopted two distinct types in protecting the grave goods with in the terracotta ring (plate XXI) structures. In one case stone slab was used like as a capstone (plate XXI a) whereas terracotta ring pieces (plate XXII b) in other type to protect the grave furnishes. In both cases, similar architecture has been noticed with little variation in pot types. A long neck pot was a new added typology in grave goods of under the stone slab furnishes. Similar type of globular vases, one with spout and cooking vessels are very common shapes in food offering earthen wares.

In TCR 08 II ring structure, two well dressed sand stone blocks were noticed. One was arranged in horizontal position and other laying down in vertically with in the terracotta rings (Plate XXII a & c). All the grave goods were arranged under the horizontally placed cap stone.

Slabbed cists are a general practice in grave structure in the region under study in different types and sizes. The cists are usually encircled by one or more big stone circles and covered with cairn stone, made of granite or laterite slab, completely or partially. The cists with multiple capstones were reported from many sites in the southern region.

But from the present ring structures, an almost square in shape (45 × 42 × 7 cm) dressed sand stone slab (plate XXII a) was used for covering the grave goods within the terracotta rings. In the third ring from the top a horizontally placed stone slab has been noticed only from one ring well. It is a well dressed and perfectly carved sand stone slab. On the interior surface, a vertically slant dotted line has appeared. Other than that there is no any graffiti or inscription. It resembles like the capstone in lithic burial monuments or lithic tradition with in backed ring monuments.

In the middle of second ring from the top of same memorial, a hood stone (45 × 15-30 × 7 cm) facing south, placed vertically besides the capstone (plate XXII b).

Hood shaped dressed stone blocks arranged in a circular alignment in one or two rows is another interesting practice in after death monuments of the region (plate I). It may appear in three or four quadrilateral clinostatic boulders, forming a square or round base and a truncated top on which rests the hat stone or *topical* (Gururaja Rao, B.K. 1972).

In the present backed clay monument, a perfect hood shape carved sand stone slab (plate XXII c) has been placed horizontally along with capstone on above the grave goods. Grave goods were arranged under the capstone (plate XXII d).

Another type of practice for covering grave goods was also adopted by the grave builders of the region i.e., baked terracotta ring pieces (plate XXIII). In TCR 08 I, terracotta ring pieces ceiling has noticed in the second and third rings from the top. It may be an other method adopted by the builders to cover or protect the grave goods and offerings. After arrange the offering vessels, backed ring pieces were arranged properly in two courses. Those ring pieces appeared irregular in length and medium in size. But they were arranged very carefully and packed tightly in two layers (plate XXIII a) on the above grave furnishes (plate XXIII b) and filled with as usual soil upto the seventh ring with domical finishing. It may be another method adopted by the grave builders to protect or cover the grave deposits.

Grave goods arrangement pattern

Between third/fourth and sixth course of the rings from the surface, funerary goods were furnished. Again sixth and seventh rings were filled with clay (plate XXIV). In all, five pots (plate XXV) and one or two big upper half removed globular vases have been unearthed in good condition from TCR 3a, 7, 8, 10 and 17 and broken vessels were unearthed from other structures. All pots are in Red ware, fine to medium fabric with or without slip.

From all unearthed grave structures made of terracotta ring, arrangement of grave furnishes with in the rings were almost similar. In all, five offering vessels and two rim portion removed big vases were common goods with or without other articles. The offering vessels are in two shapes. One is in round shape and carinated vase or *handi* in other category of vessel. The round shaped pots (four in all) are may be for offering food and *handi* utilized as for both cooking and offering vessel. All pots were made of fast wheel with well lavigated clay in fine to medium fabric. Among offering vessels, four are in round shape and almost in same size but one with spout. It is a well backed Red ware pot with slip upto bottom. Another two pots are also in globular shape with red slip on the upper portion and almost identical to each other in both shape and size. All these three pots are in similar shape, size and fabric with round bottom.

Except spouted vase, globular pots having an everted rim and with grooved shoulder. The red slip was applied only on exterior upper portion. In the case of spouted vase, the slip was applied on outer surface upto bottom. It is in convex body with an out-turned rim, grooved shoulder and round base.

Liquid deposits have appeared in the vases. However, all pots were filled with river soil and water, hence it is not possible to find the type of liquid. In all possibilities, it may be presumed that these vessels were used for storing liquid, either water or other drinks. The spouted vessel may be for serving water and other two similar shaped pots for different purposes.

Second type of vessel in offerings is a cooking vessel or *handi*. It is a Red ware vessel with a promptly flanged rim and externally grooved body. It is distinguished by a projection at the waist portion and round base. The cooking vessel is made of medium fabric, devoid of any slip or wash. In side the pot charred food substance was noticed. But due to the river water, evidences was completely mixed with sand and washed out. It was not possible to send for analysis. On the exterior bottom surface covered with a thick deposit of carbon. It may be due the food was cooked in the vessel on firewood for some time. This carinated vessel was utilized for cooking food to offer the deceased person or ancestors.

Besides the above mentioned complete shaped pots, two or three half portion removed pots were also noticed in the grave furnishes. One big pot (pitcher or storage jar) lower portion removed upto body and utilized to support or to keep the above described offering vessels with in the terracotta rings. The offering vessels were arranged within the big pot. One rim portion of a vase was noticed in inverted position. Rim portion they placed in downward direction and used as a base ring and kept the vessel probably with liquid along with other food offers to the deceased.

In the case of three ring structures (arranged in triangle alignment) complex, another interesting practice was noticed. On the rim of a vase placed an upper portion removed globular vase from TCR 3, 3a and 10. This rim portion removed round based Red ware vase is an interesting and important observation from ring structures. Red ware globular vase was removed upto shoulder portion and some inside part painted in black. On the painted portion human body engravings are interesting observations (Plate XXVI). Those human shaped graffiti are not only a unique practice but also a new finding. Of course, this was not a common appearance in the ring structures. Only from three structures these graffiti marked pots were unearthed. Out of three, only from one structure complete pot was recovered. Other two ring structures which were disturbed badly, only broken sherds with graffiti marks were found. TCR 3a ring structure recovered in complete shape without much more damage. Details are like as follow.

TCR 3a – Human shaped twin bodies graffiti

The upper portion removed upto shoulder vase was made of fine texture and thin section with round base recovered form structure TCR 3a. It was treated with a red slip on outer surface upto base and shows signs of indifferent firing. It is a well backed pot with metallic sound. Black patches are noticed on the outer surface of the pot with out any slip (plate XXVI a). It may be not due to different firing techniques. The potter even has not tried to cover with any slip or wash. It is unlike Black and Red Ware, certain portion only in black color like a patch. This type of black patches was not found on any other offering vessels either from the same ring structure or any other in this area.

In side the pot, on left side about 22 × 10 cm portion was painted with brownish black color. On the painted portion human sketch was engraved with sharp needle after firing. Two human faces have been noticed on the painted portion. One face in the upper portion with a sketch of body was depicted a little bit bigger in size and more prominent. The second face has been incised around seven centimeters below the first figure in with less features.

Figure I – head, neck and shoulders of the first figure were incised on the painted portion. Head raised and looking towards up of a human face/skull is in oval shape [6 × 5 cm] with a long line depicted for nose. Two small lines on either side of the long vertical line were incised in place of eyes. Three small cross line for chin, lips and mouth (Plate XXVI a) were notched with a sharp needle on the painted portion. On the upper portion of the head, raised vertical strokes (12) are appeared like hair. Neck portion and shoulders are appeared with long folded right hand. On the left side, another face of second person's sketch was incised. Even though the lower portion of the first figure is not very clear, it resembles like a sitting posture and hands placed on folded legs. Other body parts are not prominent but engraved in wavy lines in the below of painted portion. It may appear that a human (may be a man?) sitting posture with folded legs and hands were placed on the folded legs. The head was raised and looking towards up (upper worlds?).

On the left side, below an inch from face and on the above left shoulder of the figure I, another face (may be a female?) in round shape [5 cm] was depicted with less prominent lines (Plate XXVI b). The eyes, nose, etc, facial parts were incised similarly like the above mentioned figure. It is facing in another direction and body details are not known.

Many straight lines and some intersected small lines are appeared on the upper potion in the right side. There are no letters or animal shaped engravings within the backed mud pot. However the deceased kin took a special attention in sketch the figures in side the earthen ware.

This type of rough sketch of deceased was common practice in after death rituals in India among many communities. Sketch of the deceased on the ground where death was occurred or cremated the dead body (or pinched figures in clay or with rice or wheat flour) is depicting with a sharp needle or nail as a part of after death rituals.

Their occurrence ring structures in cluster and away from the habitation area further indicates the nature of the utility. It is true that demarcation between the residential and after death practices is very common from the very beginning. Further, this area has been using for after death rituals in subsequent periods with different traditions. Even now, this area is using for disposal of death, both inhumation and cremation, and after death rituals. Harichandra, god for graveyard, in granite statue within a small brick built shrine on elevated left bank of the river Vegavathi further attesting the utility of the land for similar practice.

Table II

Details of Exposed Terracotta Rings form the Vegavathi River Channel during 2006 and 2008 field seasons

S. No.	Ring Structure No	No of Courses	Measurements in cm			Filling material	Remarks
			diameter	height	thickness		
1	TCR 1	5	100	30	6	Grey soil filling, Red ware pottery, animal bones (?)	Disturbed, may be burial structure
2	TCR 2	2	60	20	5	Sand filling	Cattle feeding
3	TCR 3	7	75	15	5	Grey soil filling, Red ware globular vases, lamp, stone objects	Memorial, disturbed
4	TCR 3a	7	75	15	5	5 offering vessels, human graffiti	memorial
5	TCR 4	11	110	15	5	Sand filling	Well (?)
6	TCR 5	1	60	40	5	Sand filling	May be used in grains hand pounding
7	TCR 6	5	120	25	6	Sand filling	Not known
8	TCR7	7	75	15	5	Grey soil filling, Red ware globular vases, lamp, stone objects	Group Burials - Arranged in triangular shape
9	TCR 8	7	75	15	5	Grey soil filling, Red ware globular vases, lamp, stone objects	
10	TCR 9	7	75	15	5	Grey soil filling, Red ware globular vases, lamp, stone objects	

Contd..

11	TCR 10	7	75	15	5	Grey soil filling, Red ware globular vases, lamp, stone objects	Memorial, disturbed
12	TCR 11	5	110	20	5	Sand filling	Not known
13	TCR 12	4	100	30	6	Sand filling	On prepared working floor, may be granary
14	TCR 13	5	105	25	6	Sand filling	Not known
15	TCR 14	8	100	25	6	Sand filling	Disturbed
16	TCR 15	1	105	55	6	Sand filling with brick bats	Very huge and heavy
17	TCR 16	3	75	24	5	Sand filling	Disturbed
18	TCR 17	7	75	15	5	Grey soil filling, Red ware globular vases, lamp, iron objects, charred pieces (?)	Memorial
19	TCR 18	14	100	25	5	Sand filling	Draw well/soak pit
20	TCR 19	3	90	20	5	Sand filling	Not known
21	TCR 20	4	90	25	5	Sand filling	Not known
22	TCR 21	2	NK	20	5	Sand filling	Damaged
23	TCR 22	2	75	20	5	Sand filling	May be cattle feeding
24	TCR 23	4	112	24	6	Sand filling	Not known
25	TCR 08 I	7	75	15	5	Grey soil filling, Red ware globular vases, capstone & hood stone	Memorial
26	TCR 08 II	7	75	15	5	Grey soil filling, Red ware globular vases, grave goods covered with terracotta rings pieces	Memorial

Contd..

27	TCR 08 III	7	75	15	5	Grey soil filling, Red ware globular vases,	Group Burials – in semicircular alignment
28	TCR 08 IV	7	75	15	5	Grey soil filling, Red ware globular vases,	
29	TCR 08 V	7	75	15	5	Grey soil filling, Red ware globular vases,	
30	TCR 08 VI	7	75	15	5	Grey soil filling, Red ware globular vases,	
31	TCR 08 VII	NK	90	20	6	Sand filling	NK
32	TCR 08 VIII	NK	90	25	6	Sand filling	After 7 rings water found
33	TCR 08 IX	NK	NK	20	6	Sand filling	Damaged completely
34	TCR 08 X	7	75	15	5	Grey soil filling, Red ware globular vases,	Group Burials – arranged in quadrilateral alignment
35	TCR 08 XI	7	75	15	5	Grey soil filling, Red ware globular vases,	
36	TCR 08 XII	7	75	15	5	Grey soil filling, Red ware globular vases,	
37	TCR 08 XIII	7	75	15	5	Grey soil filling, Red ware globular vases,	

Chapter 5

DESCRIPTION OF GRAVE GOODS

Pottery

Similar type of ceramic tradition has been noticed through out the ring monuments unearthed in this area. The offering vessels are in similar fabric but different shapes. They have also maintained the typology of pots and total number of offering vessels. Red ware pots with or without slip have appeared in all the ring structures. A few Brown Slipped and Coarse Red ware pot sherds also appeared in the grave goods of a few monuments.

Clay

The fabric is made up of well levitated clay and has a thin section in the maximum vessels. However, in a few cases, impure clay mixed with sand and other tempered materials have also appeared in cross section. They were turn on wheel. They have a uniform slip mostly on the exterior body upto body curve. The bottom portion of most of the vessels is devoid of any slip. In some cases the slip has also applied inside upto the rim portion.

Firing

Uniform firing has been appeared in most of the pots. A few ill fired sherds were also noticed in some ring structures. They were fired to high temperature and burnished, resulting in a glossy surface and a metallic ring. The vessels were under river water for so many years, but still in good condition. It is indicating that the potters technological knowledge in the firing of earthen wares.

Red Slipped ware

The Red Slipped pottery gradually makes its appearance in the later level of Black-and Red ware in the entire region. This is a very common fabric in south Indian ceramic industry (Gurumurthy, S.). These are made of well levitated clay with fine fabric and turn of wheel. In this kind of pottery the slip is applied mostly on to the exterior surface, but a few cases it is applied on both sides. Majority of the pots are slipped up to body portion and some cases up to inside the rim portion. Most of them are devoid of any slip in the bottom portion. The slip is not comparable with gloss of the Russet Coated Painted ware of the earlier period. The slip is a thick paste of fine clay, mixed with red ochre to give a thick red color. When the pot is in leather-hard condition, the slip is applied evenly and gently on the outer surface and in some cases upto inner portion of the rim. It is rubbed smoothly by a piece of thick cloth immediately. This process gives smoothness and brightness to the surface after firing. This pottery is generally dated between *circa* 400 and 900 CE in the southern part of

India (Raman, K.V. (ed). 1998: 52). The important shapes that were found in the fabric - globular vases (in different sizes), dishes, ring stands, spouted vases, etc., with everted, internally grooved, beaked, collared and out-turned rims. In some sites like Tirukkampuliyur this pottery had a wide range of decorations by way of molded and incised patterns on the exterior rims and shoulder portions of the vessels. But in the case of Uraiyur pottery such decoration are completely absent in the Red Slipped ware (Raman, K.V. (ed). 1998: 52-53).

In the present grave offering vessels are not showing any decoration and maintained the uniform typology in all structure in the entire area. However, in some cases the incised marks are noticed on the exterior surface of the sherds. Considerably a good number of sherds were found with graffiti marks from the ring well structures. The symbols range from small lines to complex designs. However, most of them are fragmentary and found on the broken pieces of pottery. Detail description about graffiti marks have been incorporated in the graffiti section.

Brown Slipped ware

A limited quantity of Brown Slipped ware was found in the offering vessels. Body portion removed upto shoulder, vase's rim which was used as a ring stand for food offering vessel is a typical variety in this category of earthen ware. A good number of broken sherds were found from the ring structures. The entire range is wheel made and treated with a brown slip on exterior and inside the rim. The fabric is fine to medium in a majority of cases but a few coarse variety sherds also found. The glittering surface has appeared, may be due to burnish in leather hard condition before firing.

Coarse Red ware

A few Coarse Red ware sherds and part of pots were noticed from the terracotta ring structures. It is a dull Red ware made of impure clay mixed with sand and grass. The surface is rough but uniformly fired. The shapes were mostly big globular pots and vessels. Coarse Red ware occurred predominantly in the later phases from all the sites of south India. Though this pottery type is available in all levels from the most of the Early Historical sites in the region, they tend to predominate after fourth century CE (Raman, K.V. (ed). 1988).

Pottery types

Globular vases in different sizes and some with spouts, *hundi*/ cooking vessel, etc., are frequently occurred offering and cooking vessel types (plate XXV) from the mud mould backed rings structures. Upper portion removed big pots appeared to furnish the grave offers and big pot pieces used to cover the offerings. Lamp, lid, etc., earthen wares were also added in the grave furnishes of some structures.

Globular vase

Out of five offering vessels in the terracotta ring structures, two globular vases with almost same in measurements have been appeared in all structures. Third one was removed upto body portion. Rim and neck portion up to body curve was removed and painted upto some inside portion vase with human graffiti.

Spouted vase

Spouted vase in spherical shaped body is third offering vessel in the grave goods within the terracotta ring structures. It is also similar to the above mentioned vases in size and shape but with a spout at just below the neck portion. Spouts in different shapes were also noticed (plate XXX) from the damaged structures.

In the case of globular vases including spouted, the red slip has been noticed up to body portion and flatter bottom portion is devoid of any slip. These pots are with flared rim, convex body and grooved below the neck and common feature among all offering globular vessels within the ring structures in the area.

Hundi or cooking vessel

A cooking vessel (*hundi*) with a thick coke deposit on the outside bottom and charred food strains inside have appeared in the grave offering vessels (plate XXIX). From a ring structure, cooking vessel with lid has also noticed. It may be found that the *hundi* or cooking vessel utilized for both cooking and offering the food.

Ring stands

Rim portion of pots were used as ring stands (plate XXXIV). Ring stands with concave sides and featureless rim are common objects in Red ware during Early Historical appendage. Many ring stands in Red Slipped ware, Coarse Red ware were reported from the Early Historical sites like Uraiyur, Alagankulam, etc., in Tamil Nadu.

Other typical shapes in Earthen ware

Lid - A heavy weight and well backed lid in Red ware with slightly sharpened rim and slightly pronounced flange at the waist was found from TCR 10. It has a sagger based flat top in 12 cm inner diameter with 3.5 cm deep.

Lamp (plate XXXV b), well backed, made of well levigated clay in Red ware [7.5 cm in diameter] has been noticed from a ring structure.

The above described objects were unearthed from a few specific structures, apart from usual earthen of cooking and serving vessels.

Stone Objects

From two terracotta ring structures, TCR 3 and TCR 10, stone objects were noticed apart from usual offering vessels in grave furnishes.

Three stone objects were traced from the TCR 3 ring structure. They are – skin rubber [12 × 5.5 × 3.5 cm] of sand stone (plate XXXV a), scraper (plate XXXI b) of crypto crystalline silica [8 × 5 × 1.5 cm] and round [5.5 cm in diameter] pebble with little flatter base (plate XXXI c). These stone objects have been found only from one ring well (TCR 3), apart from usual cooking and serving pots. Those objects may be used by the deceased when he/she was alive.

From TCR 10 another three stone objects were noticed. These are however, in heavy and big in size. Three stone objects [plate XXXVI] are in different shapes and composition. One is in an oval shape (18 × 13 × 3.5 cm) with ruff surface. It may be used for grinding of sandal or turmeric or other herbals. A half broken pebble (10 × 12 × 6 cm) with a little tapered end which is providing a good grip to hold, an other interesting stone object from the same ring memorial. It may be used for crushing nuts or herbals. A broken granite stone (17 × 17 × 3.5 cm) with smooth surface was third stone object within the ring structure. Similar type of grinding and crushing stone objects were also reported from Megalithic sites of South India (Gururaja Rao, B.K.1972).

Other Objects from ring structures

Unidentified iron objects, (probably nail and knife?) were noticed from TRW 3, 10 and TCR 08 III rings structures. These objects were completely in corroded condition and broken into small pieces. From TCR 10, some charred wood or bone pieces (?) were found. Rings and grave goods were disturbed and broken into many pieces. Broken Red ware sherds with graffiti marks on the surface and a few sherds with incised lines on painted inside portion of Red Ware sherd (12 × 8 cm) are interesting findings from this memorial. The incised lines on painted portion resembles like the above described human graffiti (Fig).

Brick structures

A small brick built structure (plate XXXIII) was noticed in the river bed. Very near to TCR 10 ring structure, a brick built with lime mortar structure was noticed in the river sand. It is in 110 cm square structure in five curses, some bricks were missing. It is in badly damaged condition and function may be for sitting or to perform rituals or offering food for birds. The brick size is 18 × 20 × 6 cm.

Statue of Harichandra (God of graveyard)

Two small brick built cells with lime mortar have noticed in different areas on the left bank of the river Vegavthi. These shrines are dedicated to Lord Harichandra, the God or protector of graveyard. One is very near to the present village at Pillayarpallem pulitopu and on the left bank of the river Vegavthi. Other shrine has noticed little bit away from the above and very near to the ring structures on the same side. It may also be presumed that the upstream area was used earlier for after death practices. Now the area is completely abounded and the shrine also appeared in badly damaged condition. Moreover, on the same side, in the down stream, modern inhabitants are performing after death rituals.

Old shrine

Very close to the ring structures, on the left bank of the river Vegavathi a standing male human stone carving (plate XXXIV) locally popular as Harichandra (God of graveyard) in a small shrine has appeared in ruin condition. It is a brick built small shrine (1.5 × 1 m) with lime plaster. Now, the shrine's three side walls are almost collapsed and with out any roof or shelter. A small triangular niches are found on the side walls. The carved stone slab is also tilted to a side but intact. Statue was carved on a flat stone slab in standing posture with a stick holding on both hands across the body. It was carved in a granite stone with flat back. It is a rectangular block (80 × 50 × 15 cm) with flat base and semicircular finish at top. The standing male figure was carved on a pedestal with straight left leg and crossed folded right leg. The upper portion of the stick holds with the right hand to raise upto head and lower portion with left hand near at thigh. Perfect carving has appeared with ornaments at ear, neck, arms, wrist and ankles. Lower portion covered upto thigh portion with dhoti and tie with waist belt. Big opened eyes, long ear lobs and thick mustache have appeared on round face. Head dressing is not more prominent.

The occurrence of the statue near the terracotta ring structures, is further attesting that the area was used for death rituals. The modern settlements are using little away from this area, on the both sides (some modern burial structures have appeared) of the river Vegavathi, for the same purposes.

New shrine

Another small shrine dedicated to Lord Harichandra is noticed on the same left bank but in the lower stream where the modern inhabitants are allocated for after death practices. It is also built almost with similar measurements. The statue is also appeared in identical carvings on granite stone (XXXVIII b).

Similar shrines dedicated to the grave yard protector are very common appearance in most of the grave yards in the region and ritual practices and offering food items before and after cremation or burial are very common practice even now in general, especially in some communities. In some regions, male and female carved sand stone plaques, may be Lord Siva and Parvathi are also appeared.

Chapter 6

GRAFFITI MARKS

The ancient people began to sketch their emotions in the form of graffiti marks on the easily available materials like backed mud objects, stone surfaces, etc. Among all, marks on earthen ware are often found on Indian pottery in general and particularly from the most of Megalithic and Early Historical appendage. They are only rarely found on the Neolithich pottery but are common on the Harappa, Chalcolithic and Megalithic pottery. Moreover, the pot sherds in the early historical levels of the many sites have appeared along with the inscribed sherds. It may be true that the practice of scratching graffiti marks on smooth surfaces was earlier than alphabetical writing. It further indicates that even after alphabetical writing came into vogue, the earlier form of pictographic writing survived and in practice for a long time.

These symbols on the earthen ware were scratched both pre-firing and post-firing. With a sharp needle, engraved on mud pots either in leather hard condition or after backing. These scratches show the existence of single and ligature forms and small line to complex designs. Swastika, trident, ladder, triangle, square, rectangle, pyramid, circle, single or multiple straight or curved lines, etc., geometrical form; human or animal form; nature related forms like sun, clouds, rivers, hills, trees, creepers, etc., in many combination. Most of the marks are on the outer surface and at shoulder portion, neck, rim or belly in general. However, a few pots with graffiti marks on base and inside the vessel were reported.

A large number of sherds with graffiti were found in almost all Early Historical excavated sites in Tamilnadu. The sites that have a large number of scratched bearing pottery reported from the Tamilnadu are - Karur, Korkai, Tirukampuliyur, Alagarai, Kodumanal[1], Uraiyurr, Kanchipuram, Kaveripoompattinam, Mangudi, Perur, Alagankulam, etc. Some of the important sites which have yielded a large amount of pottery with graffiti marks from the other part of India are - Sanur, T. Narsipur, Feroke, Tozhupedu, Jadigenhalli, Maski, Chandravalli, Savandurg, Rajghat, Sravasti and so many.

The graffiti bearing pots have appeared in different fabrics and shapes. These are seen on the Black and Red ware, Black ware, Red ware, Grey ware and imitation ware. Alagankulam excavations have yielded scratched marked bearing Rouletted sherds (Sridhar, T.S. (ed). 2005:36). Most of them are seen only on small pots or tableware's.

The significance of these marks scholars has expressed different opinions. R.B. Foote (1901) suggested that the marks on pot may be the potters marks or owners' marks. E. H. Hunt (1920) expressed that these symbols are related to folk or tribe. His presumption was based on the study of megalithic pottery of south India. Yazdani opined that these marks have been used as ideographs to express ideas or phonetically to represent symbols or letters. It may also found that the practice of scratching graffiti marks on clay wares was probably an early practice than alphabetical writing. Mahalingam expressed that these symbols may be representative of totemic symbols adoption by regional people (Mahalingam, T.V. 1966).

An analysis of more than sixty basic symbols made by B.B. Lal (1960) shows that forty seven of them are common to the Harappa, Chalcolithic and Megalithic and Early Historic; six belong to Megalithic exclusively and eight to the Harappa and Chalcolithic combined. He feels that some definite meaning and purpose seems to be involved in them. However, so far it has not been possible to suggest any phonetic or alphabetic value for them.

Many sites like Alagankulam, Uraiyur, the graffiti marks sherds are associated with Brahmi letters engraved pot sherds. Since the symbols occurred with inscribed sherds they can be dated to some extent. At Uraiyur, based on the Brahmi letters character, the symbols are placed around third century BCE by the excavator (Raman, K.V. 1988: 82). In this contest, graffiti marks on Rouletted ware at Alagankulam are worthwhile to mention (Sridhar, T.S. 2005). Similar inscriptions and graffiti marks on potsherds were discovered at Atikamedu, Korkai, Uraiyur (Raman, K.V. (ed). 1988:69-75), Boluvampatti, Korkai, Kovalanpottal (Sridhar, T.S. (ed). 2004), etc., excavated sites in the Tamilnadu. Unfortunately, all inscriptions are fragmentary. Hence it is not possible to understand about the language and message.

Considerably a good number of sherds with graffiti and a few with inscriptions were found on the grave goods at the Vegavathi excavations also. The marks are found mostly on the sherds of Red Slipped Ware on the slipped portion and also on a few Red ware sherds. Most of the symbols are appeared on the exterior surface except in one case on both sides. The symbols are drawn after firing using a pointed stylus. The symbols are ranging from small lines to complex designs. A few inscribed sherds also appeared fragmentary and contain a few letters. These inscriptions are mostly on the Red Slipped ware and similar to other reported sites in Tamil Nadu (Raman, K.V. (ed). 1988). Some of the symbols are described in the following.

Description of Inscribed & Graffiti (Fig 3 & 4)

Fig. 3.1 Intersecting two horizontal with one vertical line and two horizontal lines and one oblique line bend towards down on a Red ware sherd from the ring structure TRW 10.

Fig. 3.2 Five vertical strokes in different measurements (1 to 5 cm) in two rows with a horizontal thick line (5 cm) in the below the vertical strokes on a Red ware from TRW 10.

Fig. 3.3 A horizontal thick line (5cm) on the neck portion of a Red Slipped ware from TRW 10.

Fig. 3.4 Two horizontal thick lines with a loop below and a pair of vertical strokes on a Red ware sherd from TRW 15

Fig. 3.5 Two vertical strokes on body of a Red Slipped Ware from TRW 15.

Fig. 3.6 Two identical symbols in very thin section appeared on shoulder portion of a Red Slipped ware from TRW 15. These are intersecting two horizontal lines with two vertical strokes may be incised with a sharp stylus.

Fig. 3.7 A pair of horizontal line with small connecting stroke on the neck portion of a Red Slipped ware from TRW 15.

Fig. 3.8 A pair of vertical lines in slightly slanting to right, intersecting lines like a plus and again a pair of vertical lines little bit below the above two on a Red Slipped ware of fine fabric and thin section from TRW 15.

Fig. 3.9 Three groups of vertical and horizontal strokes on a Red Slipped round based pot from TRW 11.

Fig. 3.10 Similar to the above from the same ring structure on Red Slipped sherd.

Fig. 3.11 Irregular strokes in different directions on a Red Slipped ware from TRW 12.

Fig. 3.12 Three vertical strokes in different levels and sizes on the neck portion of a Red Slipped ware from TRW 12.

Fig. 3.13 Two vertical strokes in different directions on a Red ware sherd.

Fig. 3.14 A single vertical thick line in 5 cm long on the neck portion of a Red ware pot from TRW10.

Fig. 3.15 Similar to the above but in 7 cm long and slanting toward left from the same ring structure.

Fig. 3.16 Consist of a complete inner circle with two unfinished and an outer loop. Similar symbols are reported from Uraiyar.

Fig. 4.1 Consisting of linear small stroke (like *ra at* Sittannavasal*)* on a Red ware sherd unearthed from TRW 12.

Fig. 4.2 Looped base and widening arms and feft arm extended with a thin line towards down appears on body portion of a Red Slipped ware from the TRW 15. It is in medium fabric.

Fig. 4.3 Similar to the above symbol, but without extended arm have noticed on another sherd from the same structure. It is in fine fabric and thin section of Red Slipped ware.

Fig. 4. 4 A slightly sloping vertical with a slanting stroke on the right on a globular vase from TRW 15 and resembling *ta* reported from Uraiyur. Other letter resembles like *ma* but tilted to the right side or may be number 10 (pre-Pallava character). It is a Red Slipped ware with grooving on neck and dotted designs.

Fig. 4. 5 Two letter are traced on the body portion of Red Slipped ware in fine fabric but ill fired. A straight vertical line which is similar to Sittannavasala *ra* and other letter is a slanting stroke on the right having two lower arms making an angle with the vertical which is similar to the Kilavalavu and Uraiyur *ta*.

Fig. 4. 6 & 7 On shoulder portion of a globular vase of Red ware from TRW 11 appeared with letters in wavy patters in two lines. Some incisions are comparable with Uraiyur inscriptions (Raman, K.V. (ed). 1988: 67-75).

Fig. 4. 8 & 9 On neck portion of Red Slipped sherd, incisions appeared in two rows. Some of them are similar to Uraiyur inscriptions (Raman, K.V. (ed). 1988: 67-75).

Fig. 4. 10 On a Red ware sherd a letter like *ta* incised with a sharp thick needle. It is a well backed sherd with sand particles on both sides without any slip.

Fig. 4. 11 It is a Red Slipped sherd with letters (ga, ma, na, o, ….?) from TRW 12. These incisions are comparable with Uraiyur inscriptions (Raman, K.V. (ed). 1988: 67-75).

The letters were scratched mostly on the outer surface of the sherds. Some of them were on the neck portion of the globular vases and others on the body portion. The inscriptions were scratched with a sharp stylus after firing. The lines of a few only are thin. Unfortunately, all the inscriptions are fragmentary. However, many letters are similar to the reported Early Historical sites of the Tamil Nadu region. Some symbols resembles like numerical like 2, 7, 10, etc., of the Early Historical period (pre-Pallava character).

Chapter 7

CONCLUSION

The result of the two seasons dug at the Vegavathi river near Kanchipuram revealed many socio-cultural trends and technological developments of the region during the Early Historical period. The excavated area is situated with in the limits of the sprawling city of Kanchipuram, the ancient city and was an abode of many traits. It was one of the important urban centre in India by the time of the beginning the present era. Moreover, it was an important religious, educational, commercial and a popular urban centre in the Sangam Age. Political importance of the region has increased from Pallavas' onwards. Art and religious activities along with royal patronage further enriched the region in many ways. The present excavations revealed that a new socio-cultural trend in the after death rituals and constructions. Hundreds of backed mud rings from proportionately a small area further indicating the large scale commercial based production in potting craft and technological advancements of the potters in this area.

Using data from the above field excavations, it is very difficult to ascertain the social condition of the people in this region. Because, from the habitational area there was no important antiquities unearthed except terracotta rings. Due to the floods in the river, the entire area was disturbed by many times. Other than terracotta rings from habitational area, other human activities were completely washed out by the foods. There was no evidence of their dwellings and other utilitarians. A few tiles were noticed in the area during the excavations. These tiles were reported from many sites in the region during the Early Historical period. We can presume that the tile roofed houses may be one of the model in the dwellings of this region also. Details of other activities are not possible to reconstruct from the available data.

Techno-cultural aspect, however, from the existed data we can presume that they were more strong in technologies and cultural systems. Hundreds of backed rings produced for different domestic as well as ritualistic activities indicating that their terracotta industrial activities and large scale production. Mud rings in different perfect shapes and sizes suggesting their advanced molded technology. After so many seasonal disturbances caused by the river, the rings are still found in good condition, further indicating their backing technology. Uniform firing, well backing in a constant temperature for a long time, etc., firing techniques were well adopted by the potters of this area. Lustrous, well finishing smooth surface in different shapes further indicating their different skills in the potting industry to maintain the quality of the product. Different moulds were used in the large scale production of the rings in various shapes and sizes indicating their utility or demand in that society.

The strong rings, made of mud in different shapes and sizes and well backed, were utilized for different needs of the society. The production of massive rings in large scale to scattered the needs, both domestic and ritualistic, of the society indicating the community use of the mud made backed rings. Even though the molded backed mud rings were very common appearance in India during Early Historical period in India, but there utility was limited. The ring structures were reported as a soak pits, granaries, or draw well. From the present excavations the rings were reported not only from the habitational areas but also graveyards. The utility of the rings for after death ritual structures is a unique feature of the region and reported first time in India and elsewhere. Further, occurrence of an enormous ring structures in a particular region is not only another interesting but also first evidence in the archaeological horizon.

Grave represent only a final stage in the funerary ritual celebrated by the survivors. Early Iron Age graves often contain information about different kinds of rituals that were part of the funerary celebrations. One that has attracted considerable research attention concerns feasting and especially drinking of alcoholic beverages. Rich graves contain special vessels associated with the serving and consuming of liquid and other intoxicants. In some cases these vessels often are luxury imports such as at Yeleswaram (Khan, M.A.W. 1963) or in other cases are lavish local products. As a number of investigators (Dietler, M. 1990; Arnold, B. 1999) have shown, the drinking and feasting vessels often form structured sets in the graves. From the present rings structures, even though it is very difficult to ascertain the type of liquid offered to the deceased but offering liquid (other than water) was very common practice among all. Number of offering vessels among all structures indicating that though vary the food substance, types of offering items were same among them.

It may be true that the grave builders in this area were utilized different materials to protect the offering deposits. Various artistic forms of earthen objects were appeared in the construction of grave structures of this region. It may be due to the lack of raw material (lithic deposits) in the region, they adopted backed clay substantial objects in the construction of memorials. The material used in the construction however, may vary but the similar purpose and tradition was appeared in the later structures. The backed mud rings protection to offering deposits was another new adoption by the builders of this area with same tradition. Occurrence of capstone and hood stones within the rings structures is further indicating the continuation of lithic tradition. Graffiti marks and offerings vessels within the ring structures are also resembles the early cultural tradition.

The social position of the deceased is surely reflected in the burial customs (Alekshin, V.A. 1983:13-58). The data recovered from cemeteries suggest that there was no much socio-cultural difference did exist in the communities of this area. Similar type of artifacts indicate that the entire region occupied a particular social or racial group with little variation in cultural practice.

Large number of backed mud rings unearthed from a particular region indicating that the region was occupied by a big community for a period with similar socio-cultural system. A sudden evacuating the region may be the geographical and morphological changes in the region. A sudden swell or heavy flood in the river Vegavathi/or Palar may cause the disturbance in the society of this area. From the unearthed evidence we can firmly say that the region was effected suddenly and people were migrated or shifted to other places. There is no evidence of reoccupation. It may also noted that only single cultural phase in this region These changes may occurred during the Early Historical period probably a few centuries after starting the present era but definitely before Pallavas.

A cluster of memorials in different alignments have been noticed in the down stream of the river Vegavathi. These group burials are in triangular, quadrilateral and semicircular in plan with 2 m distance in between each individual well. In all cases grave goods, filling and rings arrangement pattern are almost same. Similar architectural pattern and grave goods denote that the deceased belongs to same family or manner of death happen in a similar event.

The variations in the ring alignment pattern can be explained in terms of disincline marker of families or groups of the people within the same society.

Different types (terracotta ring pieces and dressed block or capstone) of sealing or protecting patter for grave furnishes shows the continuation of early megalithic tradition with some modifications. Dressed flat stone (capstone) and hood shaped carved stone resembles the early megalithic practices with the terracotta rings protection (instead of *mega lithic*).

Similar typology in grave furnishes with negligible variation indicating the terracotta ring memorial architecture practice was not continued for 1very long period. It may not be a very long tradition however, it may be a modify pattern of mega lithic or new adoption in burial practice of a particular group of people in a specific period. Terracotta sarcophagi in different shapes, uran or big pots, etc., backed earthen objects in mortal practices were very common in the region during the early centuries of the present era. But the present terracotta ring protected memorials may be an extension of backed mud products or new adoption in mortal practices. The adoption may be a little bit late and a regional practice only. Still now this type of burial architecture were not reported any where in India or elsewhere. However, very recent us a similar type of ring structure with bones was reported by local people near Puduchery to Archaeological Survey of India, Southern region, Chennai (personal information by ASI staff, Chennai). Moreover, based on the grave goods typo-technologies and graffiti symbols, these were not more than fourth or fifth century CE.

Sealing of grave goods is further indicating their curiosity in protecting their offerings for a long period. The variability of the burial structures reflects differences in rituals, symbolic behavior and ideological meaning.

Different alignments in the construction of ring memorial have been noticed. In all possibilities, there may be a group or family burials or death occurred in a same incident. It may also be found that the number of group structures were very small (only three in all). Majority of the structures are individual or arranged without any pattern. Seven rings structure is very common among all reported mortal structures. But a little variation in typology and arrangement pattern of grave furnishers. In the case of filling pattern too they adopted different methods. In one patters, grave goods were protected with dressed stone block like as a capstone. In the second case, terracotta ring pieces were used for protecting their offerings. Moreover, a special sand filling has appeared in general practice.

BIBLIOGRAPHY

Alekshin, V.A. 1983. Burial Customs as an Archaeological Sources. *Current Anthropology*. 4, 2:137-158.

Arnold, B. 1999. Drinking the feast : alcohol and the legitimating of power in Celtic Europe. *Cambridge Archaeological Journal*. 9:71-93.

Casal, J.M. 1949. *Fouilles de Virampatnam-Arikamedu*. Paris.

Deva, K. & Misra,V. 1961. *Vaisali Excavations:1950*. Vaisali.

Deo, S.B. 1973. *Problem of South Indian Megalithis*. Dharwar.

Dietler,M.1990. Driven by drink : the role of drinking in the political economy and case of Early Iron Age France. *Journal of Anthropological Archaeology*.9:352-406.

Dikshit, M.G. 1955. *Tripuri-1952*. Sagar.

Foote, R.B. 1901. *Catalogue of Prehistoric Antiquities*. Madras.

Ghosh, A. (ed). 1989. An Encyclopaedia of Indian Archaeology. Mushiram Manoharlal Publisers Pvt Ltd. New Delhi. I & II.

Gopalakrishnan, M. (ed). 2000. *Gazetteers of India*, Tamil Nadu State. Kancheepuram and Tiruvallur Districts. Vols I & II. Chennai.

Gururaja Rao, B.K. 1972. *Megalithic Culture in South India*. Mysore.

Gurumurthy, S. 1981. *Ceramic Traditions in South India (Down to 300 AD)*. University of Madras.

Gurumurthy, S. 1986. The Indus script and Iron Age Graffiti of South India. *Tamil Civilization*. Quarterly Research Journal of the Tamil University. Tanjavur. 4, 3 & 4.

Hunt, E.H. 1920. Hyderabad Cairn Burials and their significance. *Journal of Royal Anthropological Institute*: 140-156. Pl LIV.

Jayaswal, V. and K. Krishna.1986. *An Ethno-Archaeological view of Indian Terracottas*. Delhi.

Lal, B.B. 1960. From Megalithic to the Harappan : Tracing Back. The graffiti on pottery. *Ancient India*: 16.

Mahalingam, T. 1969. *Kanchipuram in Early South Indian History*. Madras.

Mahalingam, T.V. 1970. *Report on the Excavations in the Lower Kaveri Valley*. University of Madras. Madras: 48-49.

Milisauskas, S. (ed). 2002. *European Prehistory, a Survey*. Springer. New York.

Murthy, K.K. 1971. The pottery making technique in Early Indian Literature. *The Andhra Pradesh Journal of archaeology*. I: 73-77.

Nilakanda Sastri, K.A. 1976. *A History of South India.* University of Madras. Madras.

Pande, B.M. 1966. Ring wells in General. *Bulletin of Deccan College Research Institute.* 25: 207-219.

Pisipaty, S.R.K. 2009. Terracotta Ring Memorials: New Evidences from South India. *Abhijna : Studies in South Asian Archaeology and Art History of Artefacts.*(ed) S.H. Jahan. British Archaeological Reports, International Series 1974. Oxford: 28-34.

Pisipaty, S.R.K. 2010. Evidences of New Mortal Practices from Southern part of India. *Boundaries and Transitions, Social Innovations in Cultural Process.* (ed) V.I. Ionesov. Samara Society for Cultural Studies. Samara. Russia: 198-208.

Ramachandran, K.S. 1971. *Bibliography of Indian Megaliths.* Madras.

Raman, K.V. 1982. Archaeological excavations in Kacnhipuram. *Tamil Civilization.* Quarterly Research Journal of the Tamil University. Tanjavur. 5. 1 & 2: 61-72.

Raman, K.V. (ed). 1988. *Excavations at Uraiyur (Tirucirappalli) 1968-60.* Madras University. Madras.

Rice, P. 1987. *Potters Analysis*: A Source Book. University of Chicago Press. Chicago.

Rouse, V. 1989. *The potters' wheel craft specialization and Technical Competence.* New Delhi.

Saraswathi, B. and N.K. Behura.1966. *Pottery techniques in Peasant India. Anthropological Survey of India.* Memoir No 13 (1964). Government of India. Calcutta.

Sathianathaier, R. 1944. *Studies in the Ancient History of Tondaimandalam.* University of Madras. Madras.

Shanmugam, P. 1983. Graffiti and Tamil Brahmi. *Origin, Evolution and Reform of the Tamil Script*. The institute of Traditional Culture. University Building. Madras: 31-36.

Singh, H.N. 1982. *History and Archaeology of Black and Red Ware* (Chalcolithic Period). Delhi.

Sridhar, T.S. (ed). 2004. *Excavations of Archaeological sites in Tamilnadu [1969-1995]*. Department of Archaeology . Government of Tamilnadu. Chennai: 58.

Sridhar, T.S. (ed). 2005. *Alagankulam, an ancient Roman Port city of Tamil Nadu*. Department of Archaeology. Government of Tamil Nadu. Chennai.

Sridhar, T.S. (ed). 2005. *Tamizhaga Tolpazhankalamum Poondi Agazhvaippagamum* (in Tamil). Department of Archaeology. Government of Tamil Nadu. Chennai.

Srinivasan, C.R. 1979. *Kanchipuram Through the Ages*. Agam Kala Prakashan. Delhi.

Yazdani, G. 1917. Megalithic Remains of the Deccan - a new feature of them. *Journal of the Hyderabad Archaeological Society*: 56-79.

INDEX

Vegavathi Excavations
Kanchipuram
(12° 50′ N & 79°-25′ E)

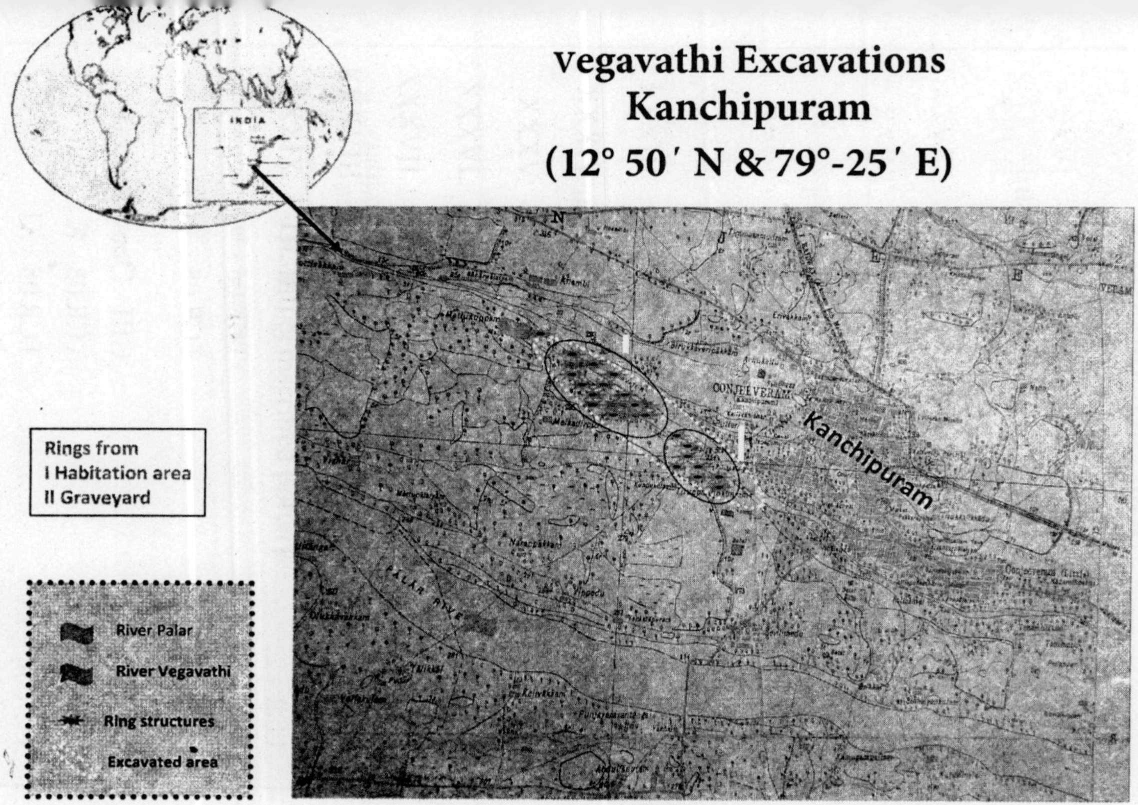

Map 1

Ring Structures

Locality I
(from habitational area)

TCR - 2
TCR - 4
TCR - 5
TCR - 6
TCR - 11
TCR - 12
TCR - 13
TCR - 14
TCR - 15
TCR - 16
TCR - 18
TCR - 19
TCR - 20
TCR - 21
TCR - 22
TCR - 23
TCR 08 - VII
TCR 08 - VIII
TCR 08 – IX

Locality II
(from graveyard)

TCR - 1
TCR - 3
TCR - 3a
TCR - 10
TCR - 17
TCR 08 - I
TCR 08 - II

GI -Triangular
TCR - 7
TCR - 8
TCR - 9

GII - Semicircular
TCR 08 - III
TCR 08 - IV
TCR 08 - V
TCR 08 - VI

GIII - Quadrilateral
TCR 08 - X
TCR 08 - XI
TCR 08 - XII
TCR 08 - XIII

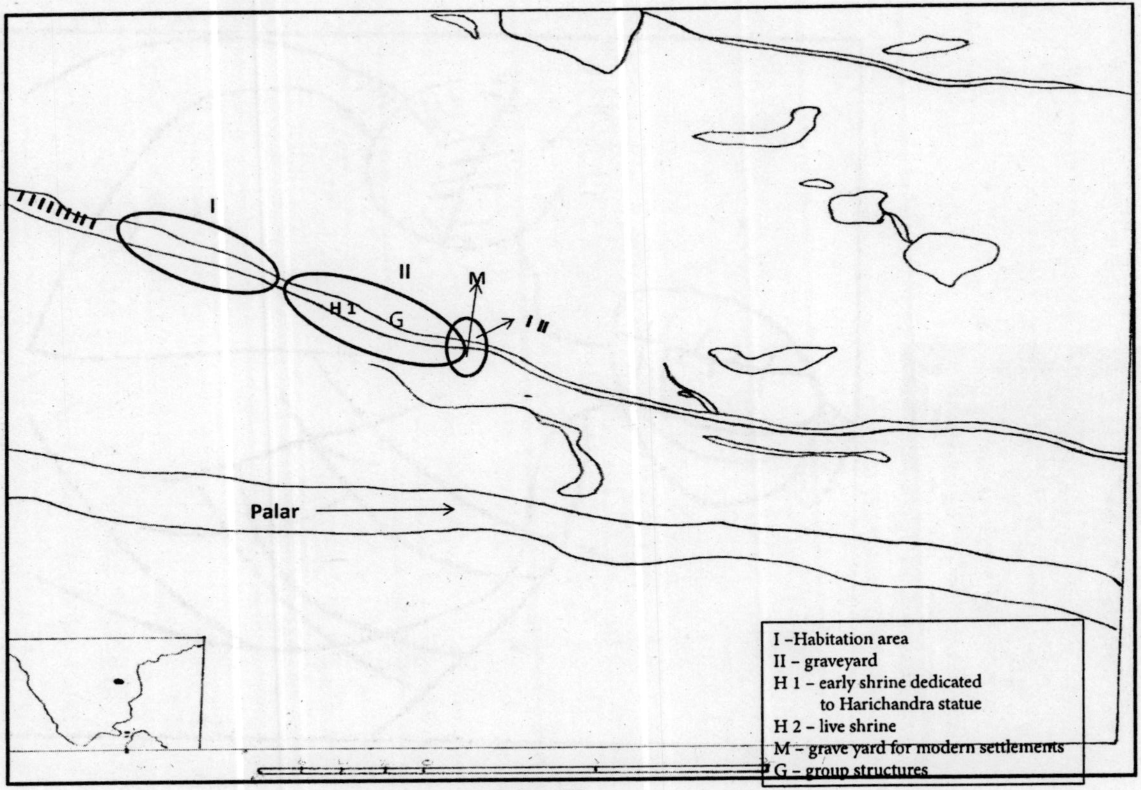
I
II
H 1
G
M
I II
Palar
I –Habitation area
II – graveyard
H 1 – early shrine dedicated
to Harichandra statue
H 2 – live shrine
M – grave yard for modern settlements
G – group structures

Map II

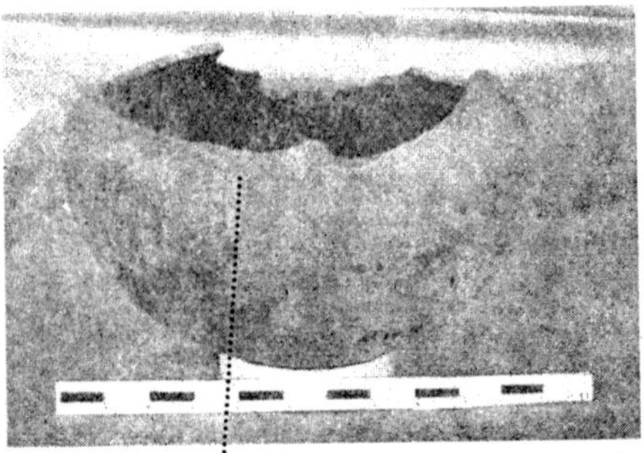

a

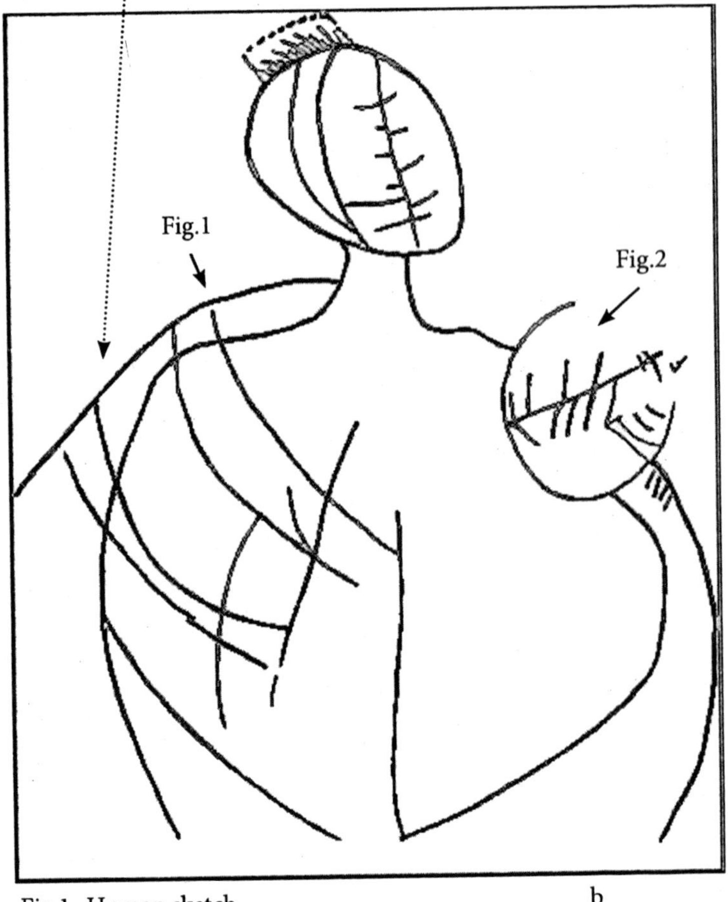

b

Fig 1- Human sketch

a. Round shaped pot with graffiti

b. Line drawing

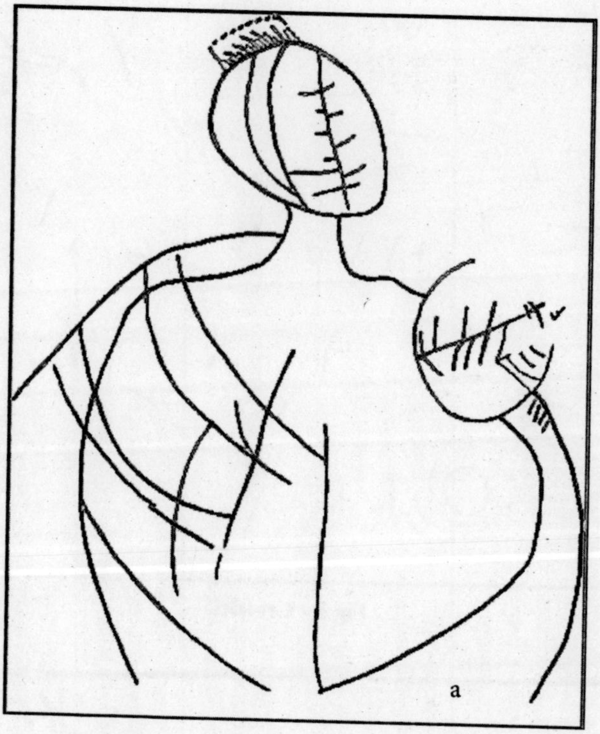

a

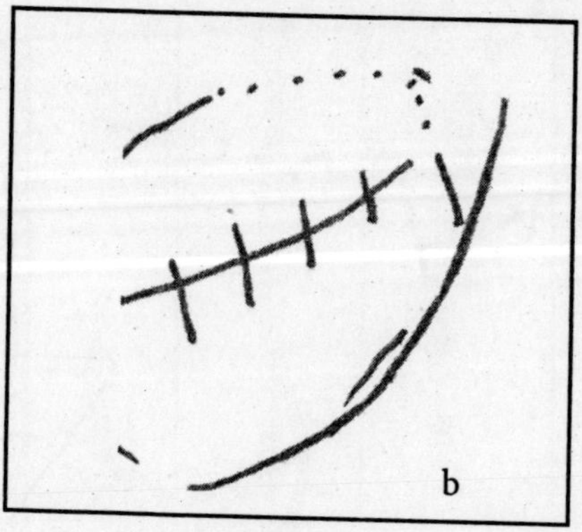

b

Fig 2- Human sketch in round shaped vases

a. From TCR 3a

b. TCR 10 (Similar sketch, but broken)

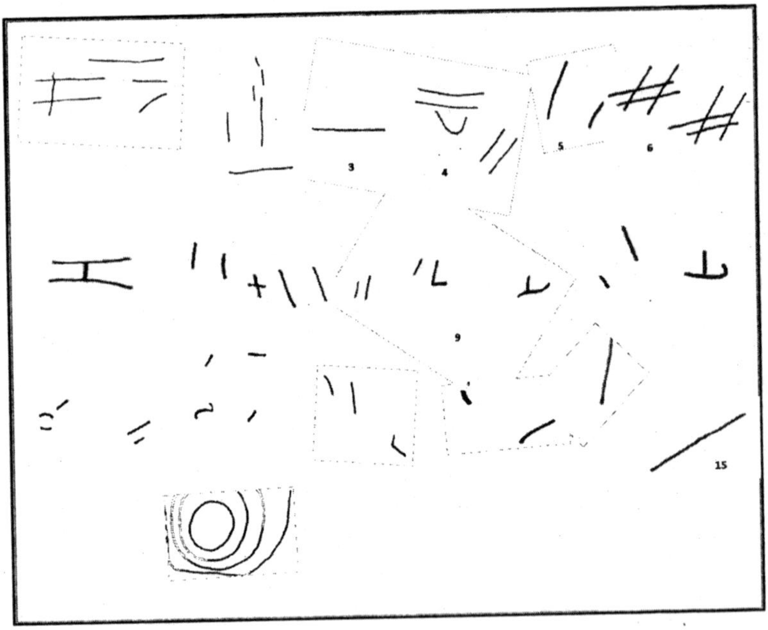

Fig 3 - Graffiti

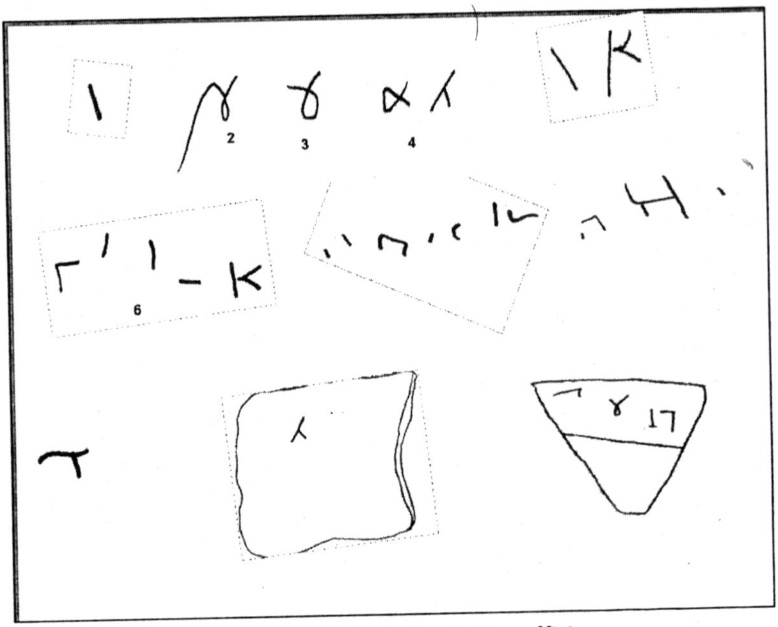

Fig 4 - Inscribed sherds & graffiti

General view The River Vegavathi

Plate I Hood Stones

Plate II Terracotta legged sarcophagus (Gururaja Rao, B.K. 1972)

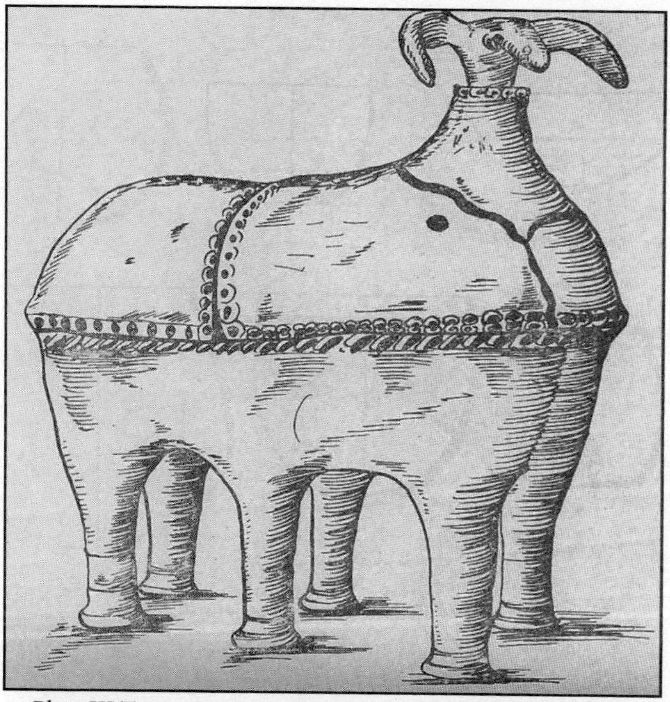

Plate III Terracotta Sarcophagus (Gururaja Rao, B.K. 1972)

Plate IV Terracotta Sarcophagus with lithic protection (Gururaja Rao, B.K. 1972)

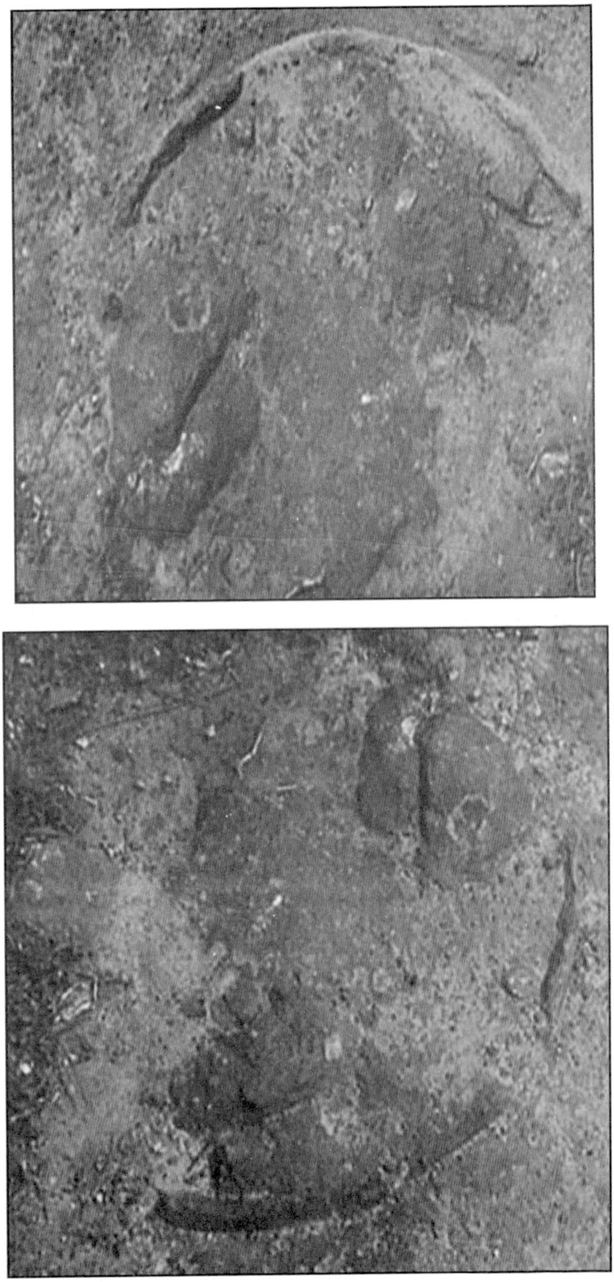

Plate V Urn Burials from Vadamangalam near Kanchipuram

Plate VI TCR 5 - Ring with perforation on both sides

a

b

c

Plate VII a & b - Hand pounding
c – single ring from excavations

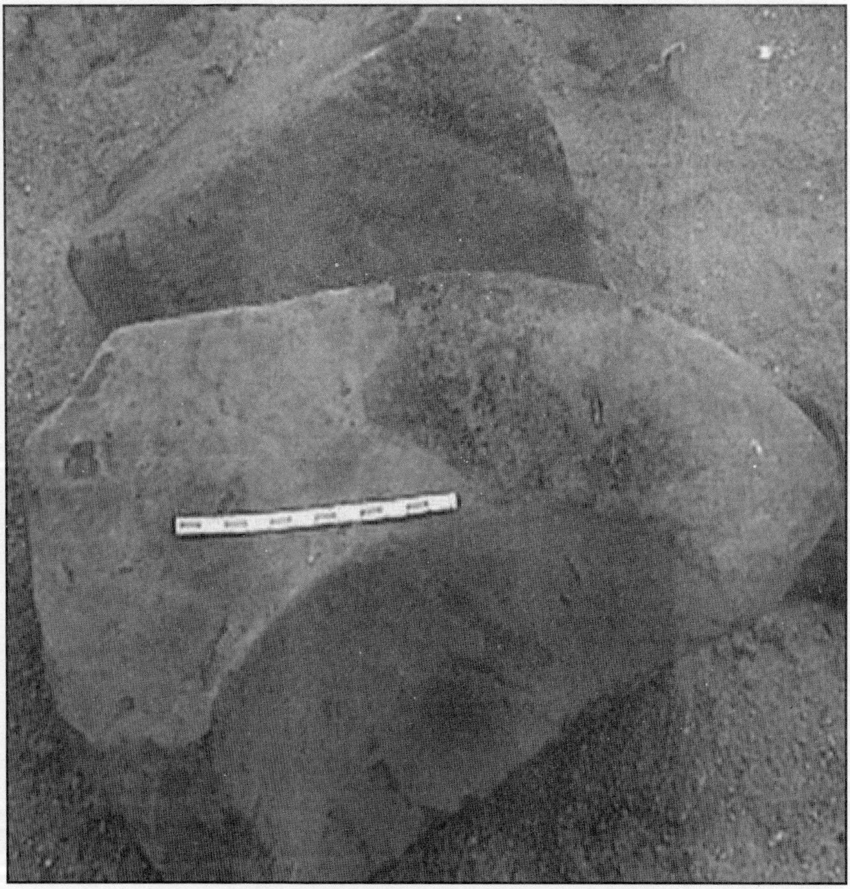

Plate VIII Pounding Stone

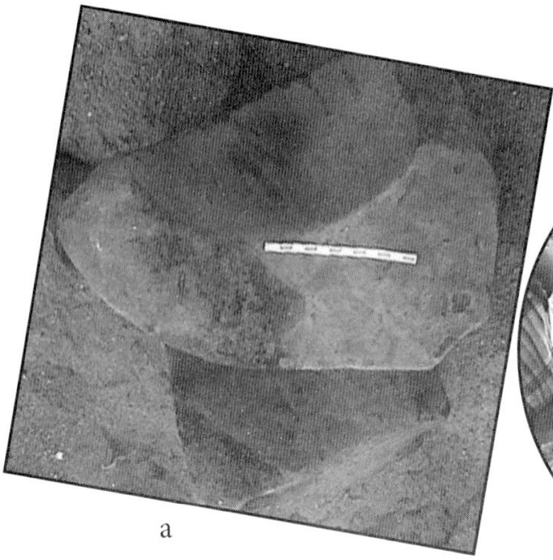

a

b

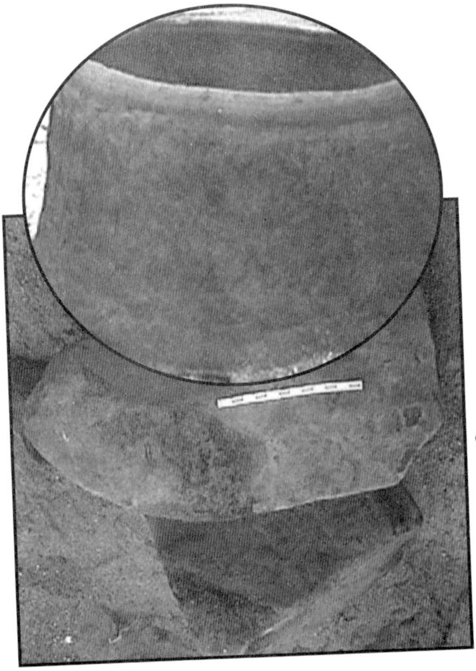

c

Plate IX
(a) Stone with depression
(b) Ring with perforation
(c) Ring on stone (pounding)

Plate X TCR 15 - Huge ring

Plate XI TCR -2 - Two Rings

Plate XII TCR 16 Rings in three courses

Plate XIII TCR 12 - Granary

Plate XIV TCR 08VIII- Rings with water

Plate XV TCR 14 – Rings in 14 courses

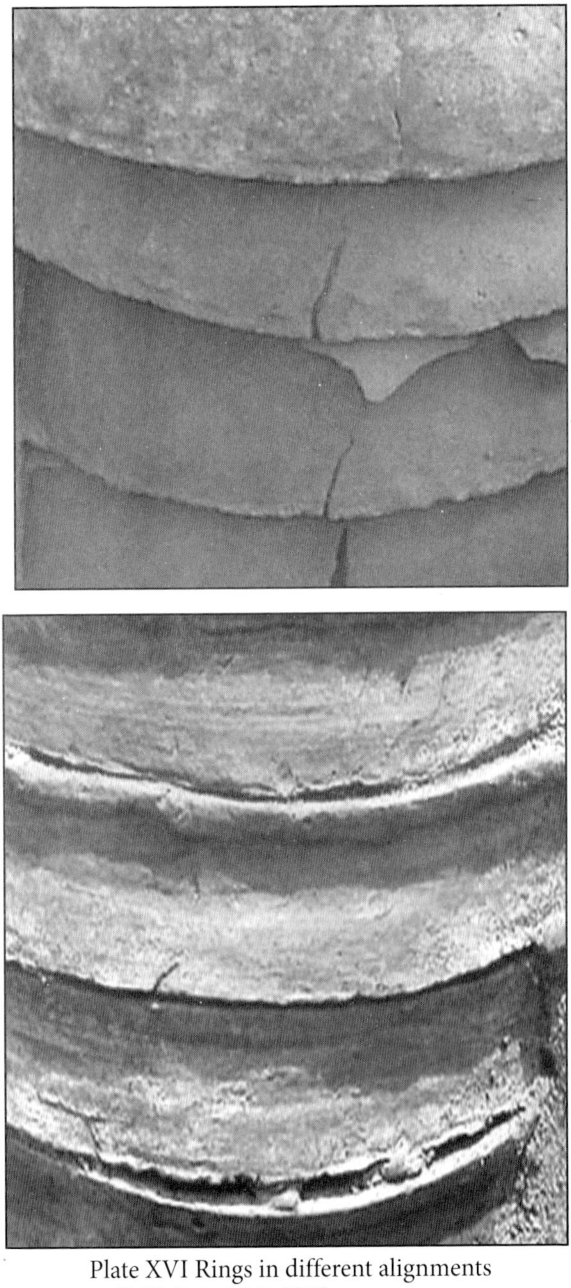

Plate XVI Rings in different alignments
a. TCR 3, 3a,10 & 08 II
b. Other all ring structures

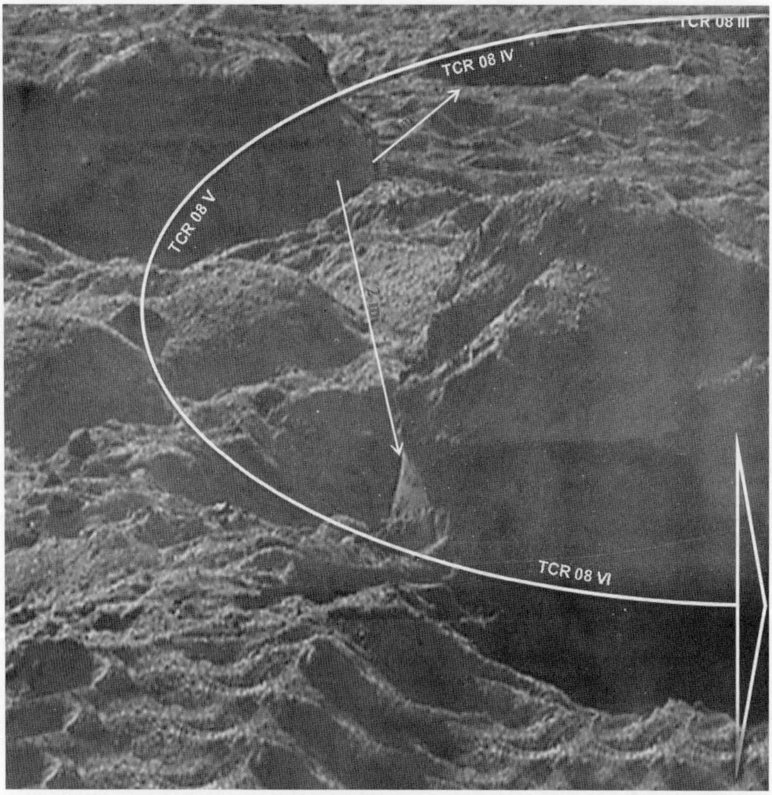

Plate XVII TCR 08 III to IV
Cluster of memorials in semicircular alignment

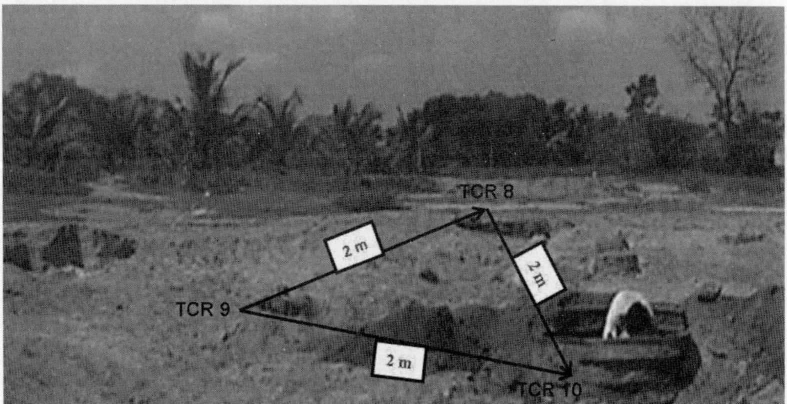

Plate XVIII TCR 8, 9 & 10
Cluster of three Memorials in triangle alignment

Plate XIX TCR 08 X to XIII In quadrilateral alignment

Plate XX Terra Ring Structure Domical shape top filling

a. Ring pieces ceiling in 2 layers

b. Capstone along with a hood stone

c

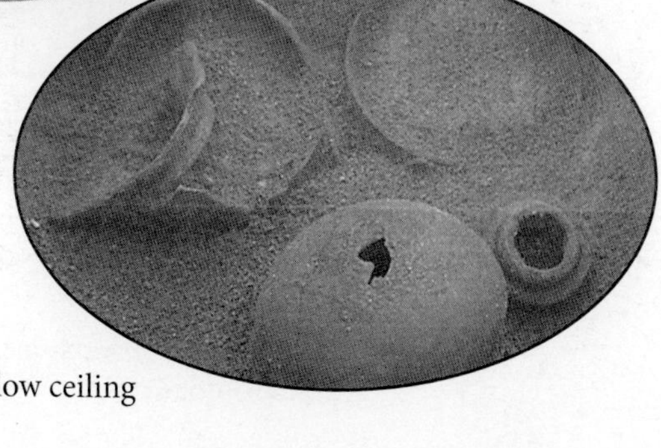

d

Plate XXI
c & d. Grave goods below ceiling

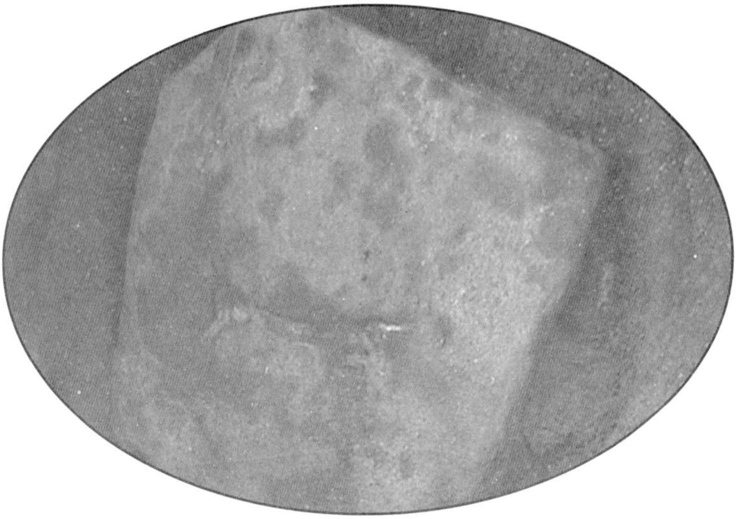

a

b

c

Plate XXII TCR 08 I
a. Capstone
b. Capstone & hood stone
c. Hood stone

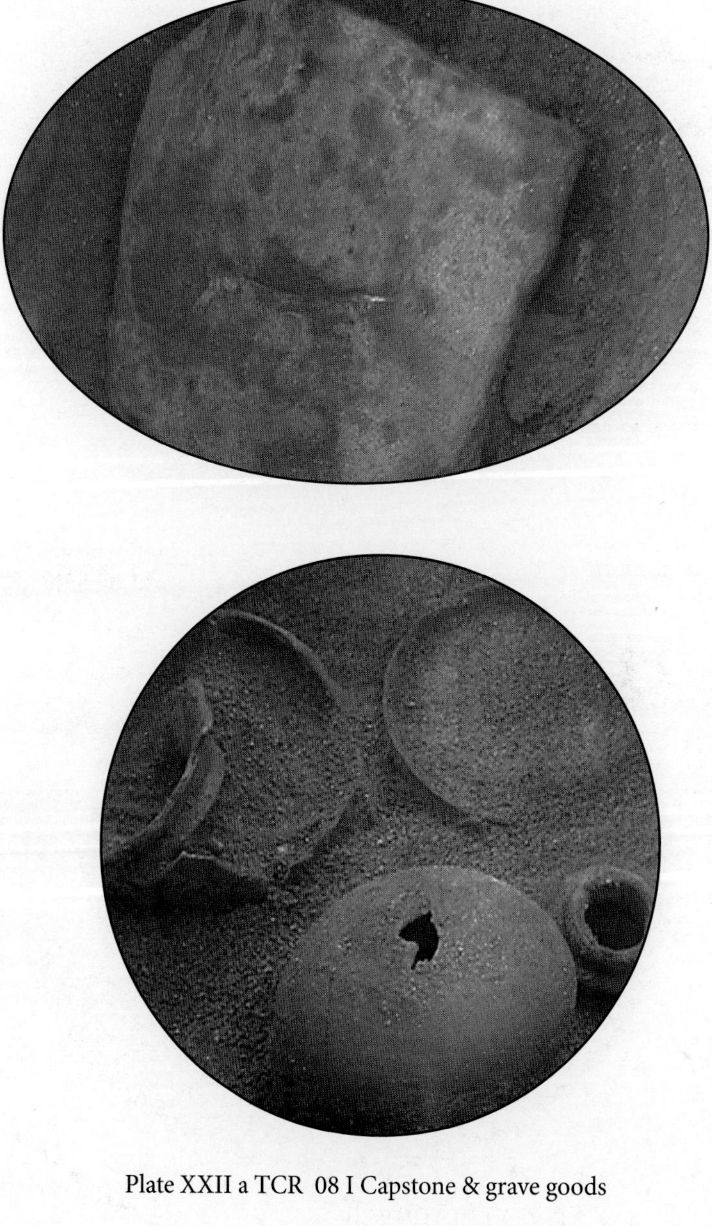

Plate XXII a TCR 08 I Capstone & grave goods

Plate XXIII TCR 08 II
Terracotta Ring Pieces sealing & Grave goods

Plate XXIV Grave Goods with in Terracotta Rings

a

c

b

d

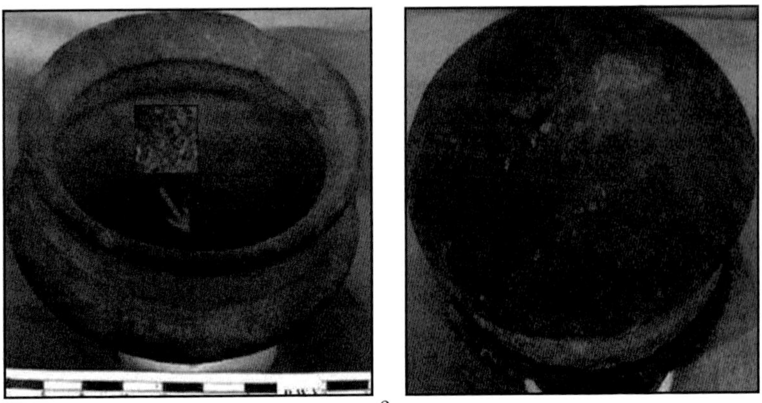

e

Plate XXV Offering vessels with in the Rings
a. Spouted vase
b. Half removed vase
c & d globular vases
e. Cooking vase, inside & out side

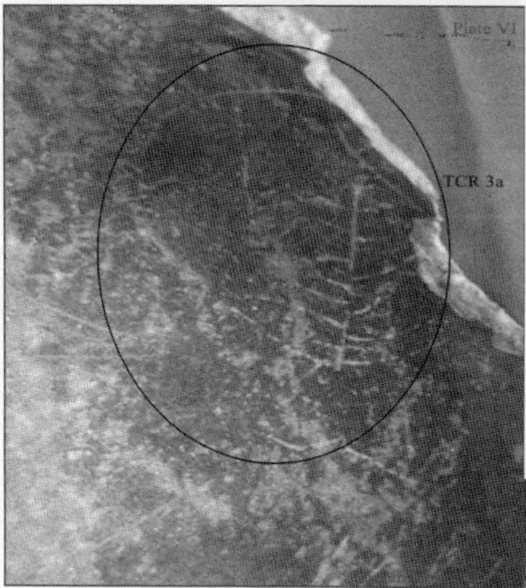

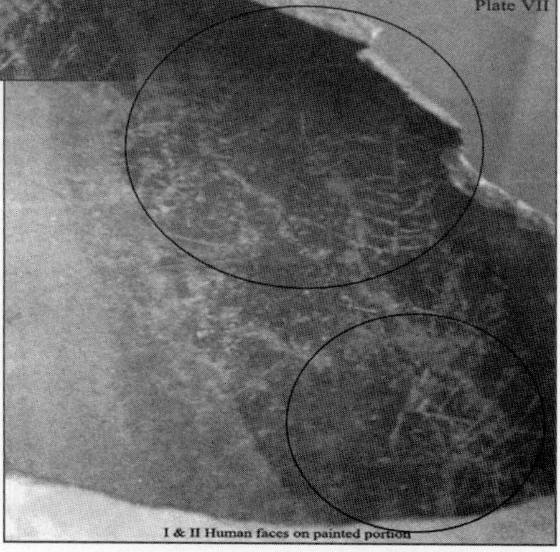

Plate XXVI TCR 3a
Human Figurines
a. Vase human figurine
b. Fig I
c Fig II

Plate XXVII Terracotta Memorial in section

Plate XXVIII Offering vessels with in the Rings

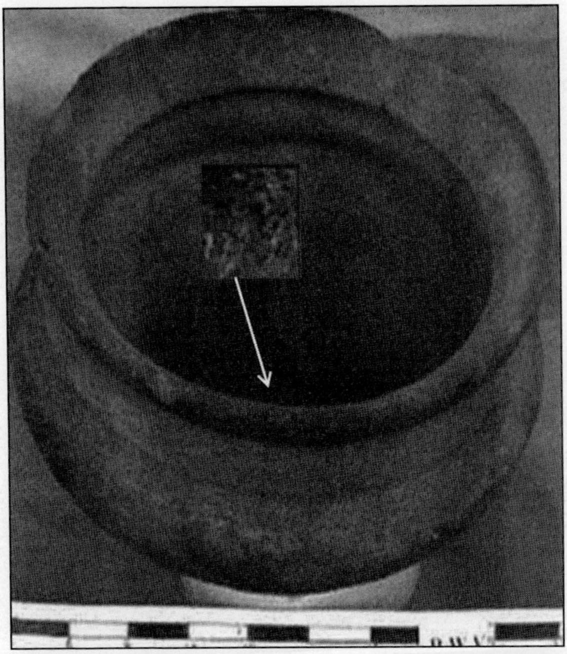

a

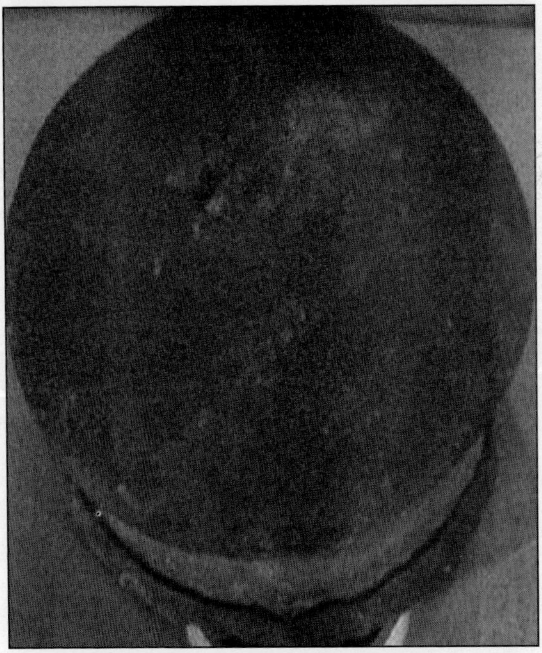

b

Plate XXIX Cooking vessel/*Handi*
a. Charred Food b. coke

Plate XXX Spouts from Ring Monuments

Plate XXXI Offering vessels covered with pot sherds

Plate XXXII Offering vessel covered with brick

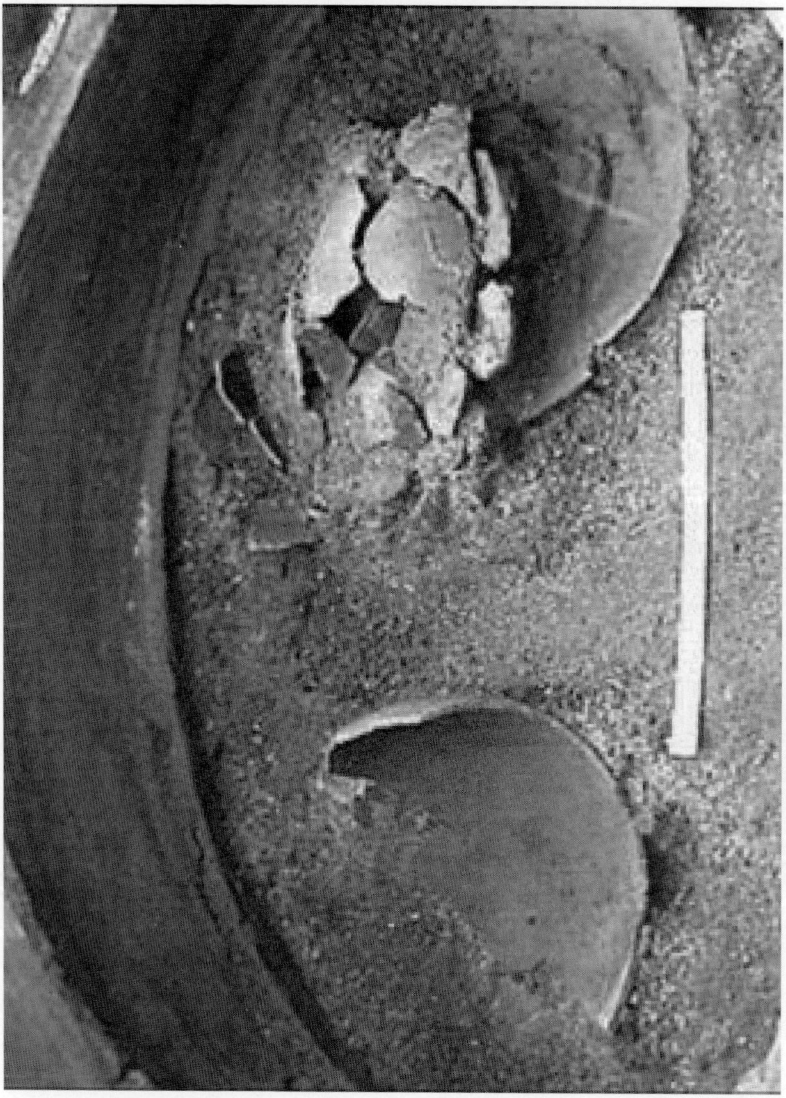

Plate XXXIII Offerings vessels with in a half removed big pot

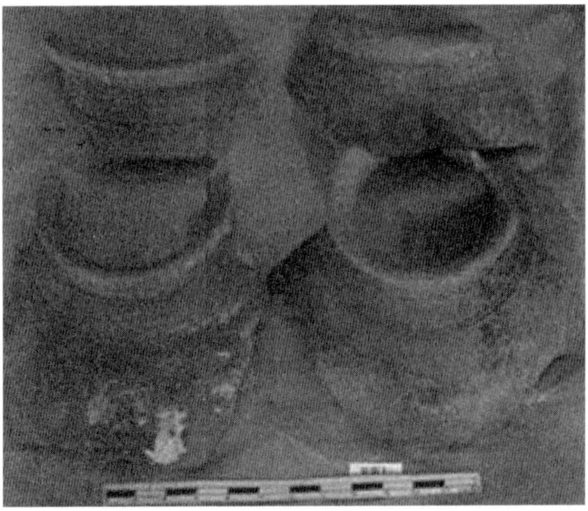

a

Rims used as Ring Stands

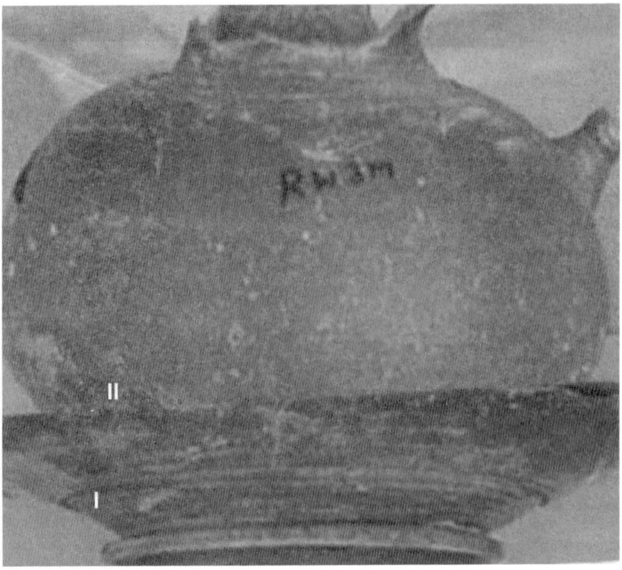

b

Plate XXXIV
a. Rims from grave furnishes
b. Spouted vase on rim stand

Plate XXXV TCR 8 Stone objects & lamp

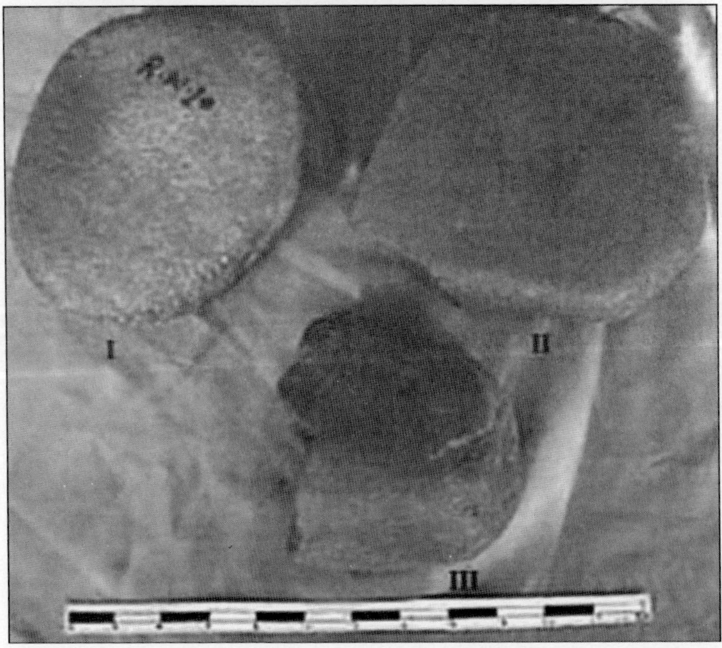

Plate XXXVI TCR 10 Stone Objects

Plate XXXVII Brick structure 110 X 110 cm

Plate XXXVIII
Harichandra
a. Near Ring Structures
(from Excavations)

Plate XXXVIII Harichandra
Recent Built (On the left bank of the river Vegavati)

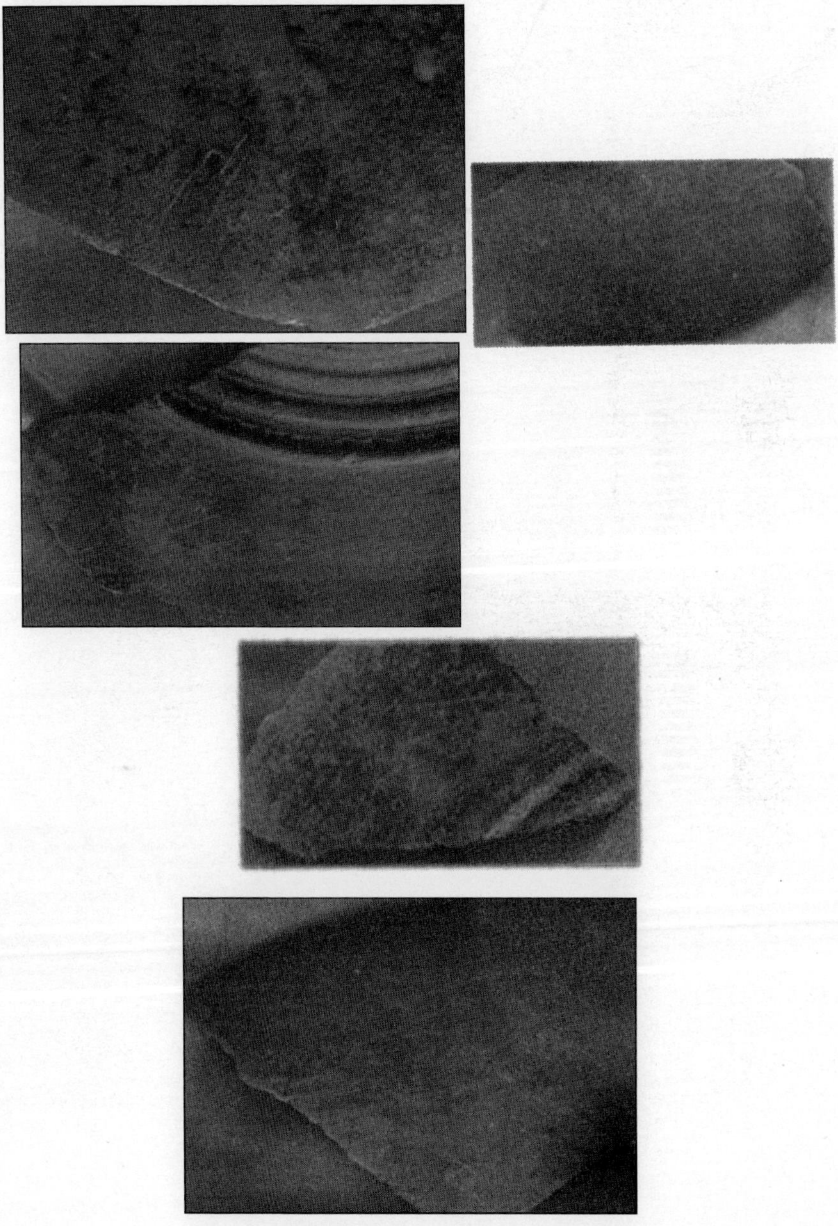

Plate XXXIX
Graffiti & inscribed pottery from Ring structures